Where Should I Work?

Choosing the Best Place to Work

Simon Moss

Where Should I Work?
Choosing the Best Place to Work
1st edition, 1st printing

Author
Simon Moss

Cover designer
Christopher Besley, Besley Design.

ISBN: 978-0-7346-1123-9

Published by:
Tilde Publishing and Distribution
PO Box 72
Prahran VIC 3181, Australia
Tel: 1300 880 935
www.tup.net.au

Contents

Preface

Most people have acquired extensive knowledge about many topics. Some individuals, for example, know that actually two moons orbit the Earth, the second of which is only a few miles wide and invisible to the naked eye. Other individuals know that bubbles in Guinness beer seem to sink to the bottom rather than float to the top like every other beer. In addition, some people know that French fries originated in Belgium, Michael J. Fox's middle name is Andrew, the pupils in goats are rectangular, the first US cheerleaders were actually men, and Fidel Castro once worked as a Hollywood extra.

Despite this wealth of information, fewer people are informed about a topic that affects every facet of their lives: how to choose the best workplace. Job applicants do not, for example, know that recruiters or managers who sit closer to you during job interviews tend to be more cooperative and supportive. They are not aware that managers are more likely to be critical and fastidious when the office is teeming with red pens. They have not been informed that recent mergers and acquisitions increase the likelihood of corruption and other illicit activities.

More importantly, they do not realize that hundreds of characteristics and features of organizations will affect not only their job satisfaction but will also influence their wellbeing. That is, in the right organization, individuals cultivate a sense of meaning and purpose in life. Consequently, they become more likely to fulfill their goals, extend their skills, enhance their reputation, and improve their friendships. They feel passionate, excited, content, and happy, both at work and in life generally.

Myths and misconceptions

This book fulfills two key objectives. First, the book challenges many of the misconceptions that individuals have formed about the qualities and characteristics of organizations that promote wellbeing and progress in employees. Many people, for example, assume they will flourish in organizations that offer enormous bonuses to reward exemplary performance. Other individuals feel they will thrive in dynamic organizations – organizations that respond swiftly to unexpected opportunities in the relevant markets. As many scientific discoveries indicate, these characteristics, and many other coveted attributes, can damage wellbeing rather than enhance progress.

Second, this book enables individuals to predict the prevailing qualities and characteristics of organizations. Most organizations do not depict themselves accurately. During interviews, on websites, and in official documents, many companies inflate their qualities. They erroneously portray themselves as supportive and cooperative. They feign concern about the family life of employees, maintaining they value balance. They exaggerate the degree to which they develop the skills, expertise and qualities of employees. They overestimate the degree to which they value the contributions of employees and the creativity of their suggestions.

This book, however, shows how employees can predict the actual characteristics – and not the purported features – of the organization in the future. In particular, subtle cues or signals during interviews, in annual reports, within the work environment, and in other contexts can be utilized to ascertain whether the organization will actually enhance or inhibit wellbeing. These insights have been distilled from thousands of studies, especially in the field of social psychology, neuropsychology, sociology, cognitive science, organizational psychology, marketing and management.

To illustrate one of these cues or signals, if employees are not permitted to attach personal items, like photos, to their desk, the workplace culture and climate is often unsupportive. Similarly, when managers tend to speak with a deep and booming voice, the work environment also tends to be uncooperative. Furthermore, if colleagues have formed thousands of friends on facebook – or if the CEO was recently recruited from outside the organization – the workplace tends to be unpredictable, unstable, and erratic.

Audience

This book is relevant to anyone who is seeking a job and, therefore, needs to decide which organization they should choose. For example, students might have been offered opportunities to complete several graduate programs but cannot decide which company is better. Similarly, this book could also be helpful to people who feel unfulfilled at work and wonder whether they should shift to another organization.

Furthermore, this book is also applicable to managers, coaches, psychologists, and human resource professionals who would like to know how to cultivate an organization that facilitates the wellbeing, progress and productivity of their employees. Finally, this volume will also be interesting to anyone who would like to develop more social and relationship skills, such as the ability to determine whether someone is sincere and cooperative.

Part A

The Rationale

Chapter 1

Do you really need to read this book?

Initially, you might not feel that you need this book. You might believe that your judgment is usually astute, your decisions are unbiased, and this book is unnecessary. You may assume that you can readily distinguish a suitable organization from an unsuitable alternative. Many people, however, underestimate the biases and ruses that may contaminate these decisions.

A room with no view

Job applicants often exaggerate their experiences, embellish their qualifications, and inflate their attributes in their resumes.

Claim: Experienced in currency exchange markets. Reality: Often travel to Thailand.

Claim: Fluent in German. Reality: Have learnt the words to 99 Luft Balloons.

Claim: Established a successful business in IT. Reality: Established a business that became successful after I was overthrown.

Claim: I have worked very hard over the last five years. Reality: I was sentenced to five years prison with hard labor.

After they submit their distorted resumes, some applicants feel proud of their capacity to dupe the organization. These applicants, however, are seldom aware that perhaps they were duped as well. They are sometimes oblivious to the possibility that organizations will frequently, and effectively, mislead their candidates. They are not aware of the ruses that recruiters and managers can deploy to inflate the benefits and advantages of their organization. Even the most intelligent, thoughtful and astute job applicants are often deceived.

To illustrate one example, interviews are sometimes conducted in cramped spaces, like a small office, teeming with equipment. Alternatively, interviews can be conducted in expansive spaces, like the board room, around a table with 20 chairs but only three people.

Interestingly, the size of this room can affect the attitudes of job applicants. If the organization was established quite recently, and is not especially familiar to applicants, shrewd recruiters will choose a cramped space. When individuals feel cramped, they tend to prefer unfamiliar alternatives. They will purchase a brand to which they have never been exposed before. They will reach novel, even risky, decisions.

Similarly, in these confined offices, individuals will also prefer a company they have never considered before. They are, therefore, especially inclined to accept offers from companies that seem unfamiliar.

In contrast, if the organization is prominent, and thus recognized by most job applicants, insightful recruiters will choose a spacious room instead. When individuals do not feel cramped, their usual leaning towards familiar organizations is preserved. They are likely to accept an offer from these recognizable firms.

Research has confirmed the effect of cramped spaces on the prevailing attitudes of employees. Perhaps one of the most interesting studies was actually conducted in a supermarket (Levav & Zhu 2009). In this study, participants were encouraged to walk down either a narrow aisle, in which they felt cramped, or a spacious aisle. The products they purchased were then monitored. Generally, in the narrow aisle, participants chose unfamiliar brands – that is, brands that were not especially recognizable. In the spacious aisle, participants were instead more inclined to choose the familiar brand.

According to these scholars, when people feel cramped or constrained, they experience the need to reassert their autonomy. That is, they want to contrive feelings of autonomy instead of constraint. To foster this sense of autonomy, they experience the motivation to deviate from conventions. They do not merely want to follow customs and traditions. They will, therefore, prefer brands that differentiate themselves from other people. They purchase unfamiliar brands and prefer roles at unrecognizable companies.

The certainty that coincides with doubt

Organizations purposely deploy many other ruses and methods to entice candidates, especially during the negotiation of wages. Furthermore, rather than intentionally influence applicants, recruiters or managers will sometimes mislead these individuals inadvertently. That is, despite their intention to be sincere, the observations of these recruiters or managers are often misguided.

One fascinating example of these inadvertent fabrications was discovered recently. Specifically, in many companies, managers inflate the benefits and qualities of the organization unwittingly. They might contend, perhaps inaccurately, the organization attracts the finest individuals in the nation. They might assert the organization is more innovative, inventive, and influential than are rivals. They might, again erroneously, maintain the organization embraces diversity and cultivates a cohesive, supportive and genuine culture.

When they begin their job, employees cherish these qualities. After all, they want to believe the organization attracts the finest people, introduces great innovations, or values diversity. However, after a few years or even months, they begin to doubt these contentions. They begin to question whether or not the employees are so astute, the initiatives are so innovative, or the culture is so supportive.

Interestingly, as investigations have shown, when individuals begin to a doubt a belief – a belief they had previously cherished – they become more inclined to assert this assumption later (Wichman *et al.* 2010).

To illustrate, recruiters might begin to question whether or not their colleagues are as astute as they had initially assumed. To overcome this doubt, they will often emphasize to job applicants or other people: 'We employ only the finest'. Alternatively, recruiters might begin to doubt whether or not the organization is really as innovative or supportive as they had previously hoped and presumed. Again, to curb this reservation, they might posit that: 'This organization is more creative and cooperative than any competitor'. They will mislead applicants, not deliberately, but merely to ameliorate their own anxieties.

The pressure of prestige

Because organizations mislead applicants, individuals are frequently disappointed with their job. They often regret their decisions.

Even when organizations represent their characteristics accurately and sincerely, applicants may still often reach misguided decisions. That is, most individuals are swayed by features that, ultimately, do not actually enhance their satisfaction or progress at work. They are sometimes attracted to characteristics or organizations that do not improve, and might even disrupt, their wellbeing.

For example, in some of the most renowned companies, the managers are belligerent, the conditions are atrocious, and the practices are antiquated. Yet, these companies somehow manage to attract countless applicants.

The problem is that some applicants underestimate the insidious effect of prestigious brands on their final decision. In everyday life, when people feel content, they are not especially motivated by prestige or status. That is, in this state, individuals end to purchase the most useful, and not the most prestigious, items and brands.

Unfortunately, as academics have recently shown, when people feel a sense of pride, their motivations often change (Griskevicius, Shiota & Nowlis 2010). In this state, they become significantly more likely to choose items that boost their status. They are, for example, more inclined to buy a prestigious watch instead of a useful vacuum cleaner. They will be more likely to purchase expensive shoes instead of a new bed.

When applicants are offered a job, they frequently experience this pride. Because of this pride, they will, often to the surprise of friends, become more inclined to value status and prestige. They often feel motivated, therefore, to accept an offer if the company is prestigious and prominent. Many applicants thus feel compelled to work at renowned organizations, like Coca Cola, Microsoft and Toyota. They often accept roles they would reject otherwise. They accept positions, despite some instinctive but intangible doubts. This inclination to accept jobs at prestigious firms is one of the main causes of job dissatisfaction

A good year

Another common inclination in job applicants tends to exacerbate this bias. Specifically, individuals tend to prefer an organization that was established many years ago. Most people feel, but often unconsciously, that anything that has existed over many decades must be sound and reliable. Anything that has withstood the test of time is likely to be desirable in some way.

To illustrate, in one study participants were asked to sample a drink. Some people were informed the brand was established in 1903, many decades ago. Other people were told the brand was established recently, in 2003.

After they received this information, the participants were asked to evaluate their attitudes towards the drink. They specified the extent to which they felt the taste was favorable and desirable. If participants were informed the brand was established in 1903 rather than 2003, they were more likely to enjoy the drink (Eidelman, Crandall & Pattershall 2009).

Paying for pay

In addition to status and prestige, individuals frequently overestimate the importance of wage. That is, provided the wage is adequate, further increases in pay seldom affect satisfaction at work. To illustrate, when individuals need to choose between a fulfilling role that is $60,000, or a more tedious role that is $65,000, they might sometimes prefer the loftier salary. The additional $5,000, at least initially, seems understandably appealing.

However, as systematic investigations have shown, these numerical differences, in general, do not significantly affect life. Over the year, the additional $5,000, is hardly recognized. The sacrifice that individuals accepted – in this example, the tedium of this role – is often unwarranted (Hsee & Zhang 2004).

Admittedly, this bias can be nullified. Specifically, individuals should calculate the weekly, not yearly, wage. They should, in the future, consider only this weekly level of remuneration when they compare the alternatives. As scientists have discovered, when only weekly, instead of yearly, figures are considered, the disparities do not seem as pronounced (Burson, Larrick & Lynch 2009). That is, the difference between $1,200 a week and $1,300 a week does not seem as pronounced as the difference between $60,000 a year and $65,000 a year. The bias towards the higher wage subsides.

The significance of insignificant similarities

Many other biases also contaminate decisions. Individuals are often, for example, swayed by trivial similarities between themselves and the organization. A man named Greg Smith would prefer to work at a company that shares his initials – like Golden Sands or even Garbage Scum – than work at another organization. A person born in 1970 would prefer to work at a firm that was established in the same year.

To explain this bias, experts argue that individuals will often, although not always, perceive themselves as special. They also tend to extend this perception to anything they associate with themselves. They typically prefer their initials over other letters. They often prefer their name over alternatives. They like the numbers that are included in their birth date more than other numerals. Therefore, they tend to assume, usually unconsciously, that organizations, brands, jobs, people or objects that share the same initials, names or numbers are also desirable.

Many studies have evidenced this bias. One study, for example, examined whether the name of individuals affects the jobs they seek. This research showed that people do prefer jobs in which the first letter corresponds to one of their initials. People called Laverne are more inclined than people called Denise to be lawyers rather than dentists. People called Denise are instead more likely to be dentists (Pelham, Mirrenberg & Jones 2002). This bias could also explain why Di Rhea became a renowned gastroenterologist, Jerry Atrick purchased a nursing home, and Jack Cass became a politician.

Because of this bias, people sometimes join organizations that do not fulfil their core needs or facilitate their development. Their reason to join the organization, although sometimes unconscious – an incidental similarity in their name or year, for example – does not indicate the practices of this workplace are suitable or the behaviours of managers are constructive. This incidental similarity sometimes overrides more important considerations. Problems are overlooked. Benefits are inflated. Decisions are regretted.

The temptation to seek these organizations, therefore, needs to be resisted. A woman whose name is Mars Bar, for instance, should be cautious if offered a job at Mars Corporation. A man called Just Dooit should not necessarily seek a job at Nike.

Not me

Indeed, countless other biases can also mislead applicants, inciting choices that individuals regret later. Nevertheless, at first glance you might feel that you could not possibly be susceptible to any of these biases. Indeed, you might even feel utterly offended by the mere suggestion that perhaps you could choose a company because of trivial details like a name. If you are, even minutely, affronted or dubious about this bias, you should consider some important discoveries.

Specifically, when people need to decide which organization to choose, they may not be as resilient as usual. Compared to other times in their life, they feel slightly, if not markedly, more fragile or brittle. They do not feel certain about how events might unfold. Their immediate future is not unambiguously defined.

During these uncertain times, to boost their pride and to curb their doubts, individuals often orient their attention to their strengths. They want to feel confident. They like to contemplate their desirable qualities and dismiss their personal limitations (Van Tongreen & Green 2010).

When individuals attempt to bolster their pride and confidence, some biases are magnified. For example, because they want to perceive themselves favourably, they become more likely to cherish their initials. They will, therefore, become even more inclined to gravitate towards a company that begins with the same letter as one of their initials (Brendl *et al.* 2005). Similarly, they might become more likely to prefer a company that was established in the same year as their birth.

Furthermore, to bolster their confidence, these individuals might also exhibit a tendency called the third person effect of bias blind spot (Pronin, Lin & Ross 2002). Specifically, during these times of flux, people might be become more inclined to assume they are not as susceptible to the biases of other individuals. That is, they recognize that other people can be duped by organizations. However, they perceive themselves as immune to these ruses. They assume they are too shrewd.

These observations imply a lamentable paradox. Specifically, the people who believe they could not be susceptible to biases are the people who are usually the most susceptible to biases.

So, why am I always rights?

When defensive people are informed their decisions are often biased, they tend to allude proudly to their past record. They will suggest, sometimes haughtily, that their choices have always been vindicated in the past. They will maintain their forecasts are always correct. They can always foresee the qualities and drawbacks of each organization – just like they can always foresee the qualities and drawbacks of each person they meet.

Unfortunately, individuals tend to overrate the suitability of their past decisions. That is, when individuals review their past decisions, their memories tend to be distorted. They tend to overestimate the positive features of chosen alternatives.

To illustrate, sometimes individuals might remember the jobs they have accepted and the jobs they have rejected in the past. Usually, the memory of individuals is biased towards the desirable features of the jobs they accepted. They remember the supportive managers instead of the autocratic leaders. They remember the challenging tasks instead of the mundane, tedious activities.

In contrast, their memory is biased towards the undesirable features of the jobs they rejected. They might remember the recruiter was abrupt, but forget the receptionist was friendly. They might remember the pay was inadequate but the prospect of promotions was elevated.

Therefore, when they review their past decisions, the alternatives they chose seemed more attractive than were the alternatives they rejected. They feel their decisions were judicious, and therefore do not believe they need any advice.

Many studies have substantiated this bias in many facets of life. For example, in one study, individuals evaluated a series of cars. They were asked to specify the car they would purchase if permitted. One week later, they were asked to recall the features of these cars. In general, participants remembered the positive features of the car they chose and the undesirable features of the cars they did not select (Henkel & Mather 2007).

Chapter 2

How to decide

Irrational consequences of rational thinking

How should you decide which organization to choose? Should you list, tally, and then compare the benefits and drawbacks of each organization? Alternatively, should you trust your first instincts about these organizations? The answer is no – neither of these alternatives is suitable.

Admittedly, some people maintain that you should weigh the benefits and drawbacks of each organization. For desirable attributes, like a generous wage, you could record a tick. For undesirable attributes, like an inconvenient location, you could record a cross. You could then choose the organization with the most ticks and least crosses. You could even refine this procedure, perhaps recording two ticks or crosses for the more important attributes.

This method has been branded as the rational approach. Because of this label, people almost feel obliged to follow this procedure. After all, they do not want to be described as irrational.

This approach, although methodical, is not always optimal. When individuals follow this procedure, they overlook key sources of important information. First, they will often disregard the characteristics of organizations they cannot articulate explicitly or measure definitively. They will not consider, for example, the vibe, atmosphere or culture of the organizations.

Second, job applicants usually overlook the possibility that one attribute can offset or amplify other benefits or drawbacks. Applicants might, for example, prefer organizations in which managers send emails to communicate information rather than convene meetings or write notes. Unfortunately, emails increase the likelihood of dishonesty and, therefore, can ultimately damage trust and inhibit cooperation (Naquin, Kurtzberg & Belkin 2010).

Indeed, because of this complication, attributes that initially seem pleasing could actually be detrimental. Attributes that initially seem unwelcome might actually be desirable. Usually, for example, applicants might feel that a heavy workload is particularly undesirable. However, when employees are granted autonomy and support, a heavy workload can actually be quite uplifting (Karasek 1979).

Third, specific attributes might translate to both benefits and drawbacks, but at different times. For example, the workgroup might seem insular at first, reluctant to welcome and embrace newcomers. This inhospitable behaviour is initially disconcerting. However, over time, individuals might become an entrenched member of this exclusive clique. They might feel especially secure and stable.

Fallible instincts

So, when people collate and compare the benefits and drawbacks of each organization, they often neglect telling information. Their choices, therefore, are often misguided.

Other people, including many authors, instead contend that people should trust their first instincts. That is, when applicants meet a manager, they form an immediate impression about this person. Similarly, when they observe an organization, they form an immediate impression about this workplace. Many people assume these initial impressions are accurate. If these impressions are unfavourable, people believe they should reject an offer. If these impressions are encouraging, people feel they should accept the offer.

However, many studies indicate that first impressions are usually inaccurate, contrary to popular opinion. This important discovery was first observed in a study that examined the responses of students to multiple choice questions. In many schools and universities, students need to complete multiple choice questions. That is, they need to decide which one of four or so alternative statements is correct.

Some teachers advocate that students should always trust their first impressions. If they initially feel the answer is option A, they should not later change their answer to B, C or D. They should remain firm, even if they begin to experience doubts and reservations.

Several years ago, a team of researchers tested whether or not this approach is effective (Kruger, Wirtz & Miller 2005). They closely scrutinized the responses of students to multiple choice questions. Using a special technique, they were able to determine whether or not students had modified their answers during the exam. Interestingly, when students modified their answers, and thus rejected their first impression, they were more likely to answer the question correctly. Modified answers were more accurate than were first impressions.

Specifically, when individuals meet a person or observe an organization, their first impressions are derived from limited information. In particular, these first impressions usually depend on whether the person or organization seems threatening or not. If the person or organization does not seem threatening – for example, if the manager smiles warmly – the initial impression is favourable. If the person or organization does seem threatening – perhaps because the manager belongs to another race or ethnicity – the initial impression is not as favourable.

Emergent intuitions

If methodical analyses or initial instincts are unsuitable, how should you reach a decision about which organization to choose? According to recent discoveries in the field of cognitive psychology, rather than trust your first instincts you should learn to utilize any intuition or hunch that emanates gradually, often over a period of 30 minutes or longer.

To illustrate, in one study participants were asked to decide which of four paintings they would like to purchase. Some of these participants were invited to contemplate the benefits and drawbacks of these paintings. That is, they were encouraged to apply the procedure that is often called rational.

Some of the participants were instead invited to trust their first impressions or initial instincts. They were instructed to choose the painting they prefer at first glance.

Finally, some of the participants were instead instructed to refrain from either of these approaches. Instead, these individuals were told first to scan the paintings briefly. They were then asked to complete a crossword puzzle, to distract their attention for 15 minutes. Next, after this delay, they were asked to trust any intuition or hunch they experience. Therefore, rather than trust their first impressions, these individuals derived their choice from intuitions that evolved over time.

Several weeks later, participants were contacted again. They were asked to indicate their satisfaction with the painting. Specifically, they were asked to specify the amount of money they would accept to return the painting.

The results were stark. If individuals trusted their intuition, after a 15 minute delay, they were more satisfied with their purchase. They would not return the painting unless offered a significant fee. In contrast, if individuals had applied the rational approach, or trusted their first impression, they were not as satisfied with this painting. They were willing to return the painting, even for a modest fee (Dijksterhuis & van Olden 2006).

Indeed, many studies have corroborated the benefit of intuitions – that is, hunches that evolve over time. Nevertheless, some complications have been observed. Intuition is not always suitable.

The complexities of simplicity

First, if the decision is simple, intuition is not effective. That is, if the alternatives differ on only a couple of attributes, choices should not be derived from hunches that evolve over time. For example, if two organizations differ on only two characteristics – perhaps the level of pay and their location – intuition can be misleading (Dijksterhuis *et al.* 2007).

However, organizations seldom, and probably never, differ on only a couple of attributes. Usually, countless features vary across most companies: the design of offices, the number of employees, the strategic values, the appraisal of performance, the age of managers, and many other characteristics. This complication, therefore, is not applicable to this book. If the book was entitled 'Which pair of scissors should I purchase?' or 'Which pair of black socks should I wear today?', intuition might not be as applicable.

Vivid imagination

Second, when people can imagine the organizations vividly, they are more likely to utilize their intuition (Lee, Amir & Ariely 2009). That is, if they can visualize their surroundings, work activities and social interactions at these organizations with some clarity, their intuition is powerful and their choices are often judicious.

However, in most instances individuals cannot imagine these organizations vividly. They are not granted an opportunity to observe the activities of these companies. They are seldom, if ever, permitted to witness a meeting, conflict or other event that might clarify the atmosphere and ambience of these workplaces. Their images of these environments, therefore, are usually hazy and uncertain.

Some exceptions have been reported, however. In one example, a man had been the cleaner of a recruitment company located in Chicago. Because his role was confined to cleaning toilets and emptying bins, none of the employees ever concealed information from him. They would not refrain from discussing private matters while he was nearby. Years later, when he did eventually apply to become a recruiter and arrived in an elegant suit, nobody recognized him. They were shocked, however, by the remarkable insights he seemed to have acquired about the organization and therefore was awarded the role immediately.

To override this problem, you could undertake a series of activities that have been shown to evoke more vivid images. To illustrate, suppose you need to decide between two organizations. You should imagine, for a few minutes, that you are beginning work at each organization tomorrow. That is, imagine awakening tomorrow, preparing yourself before work, arriving at the organization, and then completing your first day. Envisage the tasks you might complete and the conversations you might begin. For each organization, imagine that people are friendly and managers are supportive.

After individuals complete these exercises, their images of the organization tend to be more vivid and detailed. That is, the organization is not merely an abstract, theoretical concept but an actual, tangible entity.

Furthermore, if possible, you should actually observe as many rooms and offices in the organization as possible. After a job interview, for example, you could ask whether or not you could use the toilet. Sometimes, as you proceed towards the toilet, you will be granted the opportunity to stroll through various corridors and rooms, enabling a more comprehensive scrutiny of the premises. Later, after you leave, you might be able to form a more accurate image of the work environment.

> ✓ Whenever you need to choose between two or more organizations, attempt to observe the offices if possible. In addition, imagine that you are preparing to work at each organization tomorrow.

Intuition and intimacy

Third, if individuals do not feel they have developed close, stable, and meaningful friendships or relationships, they are not as likely to utilize their intuition (Pacini & Epstein 1999). That is, some individuals do not feel close to many, or even any, other people. Whenever they need to disclose their concerns, anxieties or other private feelings, they feel uneasy. Whenever they must depend on another person, they feel uncomfortable and frustrated. Instead, they like to remain independent. They undertake activities that boost their status, power, standing and prominence rather than establish warm, sincere and candid relationships.

Whether or not individuals trust other people and are willing to disclose their feelings varies over time. People, for example, might remember a time in which they felt violated or disappointed. A friend might have behaved unsupportively. A partner might have breached their confidence. A colleague might have acted derisively, mocking one of their tendencies.

These events and memories can, at least momentarily, provoke distrust. In response, individuals are not as likely to trust their intuition. They prefer to consider decisions methodically and systematically, collating and comparing the benefits and drawbacks of each alternative.

On other occasions, individuals feel some of their friends, relatives or colleagues are supportive. They begin to cherish their friendships. Their compulsion to increase their sense of power or status diminishes, at least marginally. In this state, they become more inclined to trust their intuition. Hunches that transpire after some delay often guide their choices.

> ✓ After you imagine two or more organizations vividly, identify a couple of supportive, encouraging people in your life: a friend, relative or partner, for example. Reminisce about interactions with these individuals – interactions you enjoyed. Furthermore, reflect upon which organization they might prefer.

Finally, you can contact these individuals. You can express your intuitions or feelings about each organization but, to maintain awareness of these hunches, do not justify these evaluations or analyse the alternatives systematically.

The elusive emotions

Finally, when individuals experience negative emotions – anxiety, agitation, dejection, despair, guilt or shame, for example – their intuition is not as effective. The clarity of their hunches tends to decline. At one time, they experience a preference towards one organization. Moments later, they experience an aversion towards this organization. They cannot be certain which of these intuitions is correct and therefore feel unconfident and uncomfortable (Baumann & Kuhl 2003).

In one sense, the solution is simple: job applicants should improve their mood before they trust their intuition. They should undertake any activity that evokes positive emotions: they could walk in a park, meditate in the bath, relax in the sun, breathe deeply, listen to their favourite uplifting music, attend a party, watch a comedy, indulge in a book, perform a vigorous activity, or organize their house.

Nevertheless, these attempts are not always successful. Activities that are supposed to evoke positive emotions sometimes evoke negative feelings instead, at least after a delay. That is, in general people overestimate the benefits of activities or events that are intended to enhance their mood. They expect to feel substantially better after they undertake these activities, called the affective forecasting bias. In practice, however, their mood often improves only marginally and fleetingly (Wilson & Gilbert 2003, 2005).

Specifically, many of these exercises, despite their momentary benefits, provoke a series of complications. In quiet locations – perhaps in the park, bath or sun – individuals sometimes ruminate. They fixate on some of their problems, anxieties and concerns, occasionally escalating into panic and dread (Van Dillen & Koole 2007).

In uplifting environments, perhaps exciting parties or comedic movies, individuals sometimes feel so miserable in comparison to everyone else. They contrast the dejection or despair they feel with the excitement and joy of other people. This contrast can amplify their shame and intensify unpleasant emotions. These negative emotions, unfortunately, magnify this tendency of individuals to compare themselves to other people (Avramova & Stapel 2008). These contrasts, therefore, are reinforced and their mood sometimes plummets.

Even activities that circumvent these problems can evoke other complications. When individuals indulge in a book, they often experience a sense of uncertainty and suspense. They are not certain how the plot will unravel. They are not sure, for example, which events will befall the protagonists. Interestingly, these feelings of uncertainty, even about a trivial issue, actually amplify the emotions of individuals (Wilson *et al.* 2005). Mild feelings of anxiety can translate into intense apprehension. Mild feelings of dejection can escalate into utter despair.

Even if these problems do not transpire – even if these activities seem to enhance mood – intuition might still be impeded. Specifically, after undertaking some activities, such as strolling through a park, individuals sometimes believe their mood has improved. They maintain that their anxiety or dejection has dissipated.

However, in some instances, this belief is misguided. These individuals have, perhaps, actually obscured their genuine emotions. They have managed to conceal these negative feelings, even from themselves.

Many studies verify this possibility (Quirin *et al.* 2009). That is, in many instances individuals maintain their mood has improved. When asked, they claim to feel happy, excited and content, for example. Measures that gauge their unconscious experiences indicate that their mood has not improved. Their blood pressure is elevated and their palms are sweaty, both indicative of fear or anxiety. They perceive everything in their environment, from patterns to brand names, as unfavourable, suggestive of unpleasant emotions.

These unpleasant emotions, even if unconscious, tend to impair intuition. These negative states inhibit the brain circuits that generate intuitive hunches.

Fortunately, some activities tend to circumvent these complications. That is, some exercises improve unconscious mood as well, often over an extended period. For example, when individuals attempt to unearth a vast array of creative solutions to existing problems, their mood often improves. Specifically, if individuals attempt to uncover odd and unusual suggestions – suggestions that might be ridiculous instead of feasible – they often feel uplifted.

For instance, in one British marketing firm the manager instructed employees to solve an ongoing concern: the limited profile of this organization. To cultivate a jovial atmosphere, employees were first encouraged to propose amusing, if not implausible, suggestions on a white board. Two days later, the manager was arrested after several police officers, strolling casually past the office, misconstrued the contents of this white board – contents that included phrases like 'abduct Angelina Jolie', 'ignite the building', and 'desecrate Westminster Abbey'.

This activity offers several benefits. When individuals deliberately entertain weird and peculiar thoughts, they experience feelings of amusement and delight (Hirt, Devers & McCrea 2008). In addition, because they accept any thoughts or solutions, even if preposterous, they do not judge themselves as harshly. They relinquish any remnants of perfectionism. They are not as likely to experience a sense of failure.

Furthermore, because they accept any solutions, they do not think as cautiously and carefully as usual. Instead, they entertain a torrent of thoughts. A rapid surge of different musings has been shown to improve mood (Pronin, Jacobs & Wegner 2008). This stream of thoughts, according to these researchers, increases the production of dopamine in the brain, a chemical that is associated with a feeling of reward and pleasure.

> ✓ Before you decide which organization to choose, you should attempt to uncover many solutions to an existing problem, including unusual or unrealistic possibilities. You could, for example, identify all the different activities you might attempt to improve your skills.

The benefits of this book

Unfortunately, until you have worked at these organizations, you cannot form an accurate image of the alternative organizations. You cannot predict, for example, whether or not you will be bombarded by conflicting instructions, demands and expectations. You cannot imagine the conduct of peers whenever the workload escalates. You will not be able to foresee the behaviour of managers whenever targets are not fulfilled. You cannot envisage whether or not the job will seem monotonous or challenging after several months.

That is, despite your endeavours, your image of the organization will tend to be imprecise and distorted. The main purpose of this book is to resolve this limitation. This book enables readers to predict, with greater precision, the behaviour of managers, the conduct of colleagues, and the attitudes you are likely to experience at the organization. This book ensures you can distil the culture and climate of the organization from a few subtle cues and signals.

For example, in some organizations employees are informed about every pivotal decision and major plan. They receive detailed summaries of audits, surveys and other attempts to characterize the merits and limitations of the organization. They are granted access to the key recommendations of management consultants. They are permitted to read the minutes of meetings in which key decisions were eventually reached. Budgets and forecasts are disseminated to employees. Impending as well as potential changes are communicated widely.

In other organizations, none of this information is distributed to employees. Managers might either deliberately conceal these insights or merely overlook the need to disseminate information.

If employees are granted access to privileged information, and this information is organized coherently, these individuals tend to feel more attached or loyal to the organization. They feel like the organization is part of their identity – like something they own. Because of this loyalty, they become more inclined to assist the organization. They are more likely to help colleagues, ultimately cultivating a collaborative environment. Indeed, as research has cogently shown, when employees have acquired significant knowledge about the organization, they are more inclined to enact discretionary behaviours that improve their organization (O'Driscol, Pierce & Coghlan 2006).

> ✓ During the interview process, if applicants received some privileged information about the organization – such as access to recommendations of consultants, summaries of audits, or minutes of meetings – the work environment is likely to be collaborative and supportive. Some employees will dedicate effort to facilitate your work.

This book will explore a variety of similar cues and signals, each validated by a series of studies. After you read each section, you should form another image of the organization – an image of a typical day. In this example, if you did receive some privileged information about the organization, you should imagine a few supportive and cooperative employees, sacrificing their own interests to facilitate your work. If you did not receive any privileged information, you should not form this image. Perhaps you could imagine a more competitive environment. These exercises will enhance your intuition, increasing the likelihood that you will you choose the most satisfying and fulfilling work environment.

Chapter 3

The model company

The purpose of meaning

What do you want in life? What qualities would you like to cultivate? How would you like to feel every day?

In answer to these questions, most people express a range of answers: they would like to be resilient, content, gifted, influential, respected, loved and helpful. They want to be happy and fulfilled.

Only a few people allude to meaning and purpose. That is, only a few people say they would like all of their activities and pursuits to align to an enduring and significant quest. If asked whether they would like their life to be meaningful and purposeful, they might reply with a shrug of the shoulders, perhaps accompanied by an answer like 'Yeah sure, why not'.

Yet, as scientists are beginning to reveal, this sense of meaning and purpose actually fosters all the other benefits (Ho, Cheung & Cheung 2010). When individuals perceive their life as meaningful, they are more likely to feel resilient and hardy. They are more likely to feel content and satisfied. They are more inclined to cultivate important skills, insights and talents. They will often, at least eventually, be appointed to positions of influence and respect. Finally, they are more likely to form solid, trusting and supportive relationships – friendships that will last indefinitely. Organizations that cultivate this sense of meaning in employees, therefore, will enhance wellbeing.

You stupid numbskull – and other impulsive outbursts

In contrast, when people do not experience this sense of meaning, the direction of their life seems uncertain. They are not, therefore, as willing to sacrifice their immediate needs to pursue their future aspirations. For example, they are not as inspired to accumulate knowledge or skills because they cannot be sure which talents and insights may be germane in the future. They will shun challenging opportunities.

Without purpose, individuals primarily strive to satisfy their more immediate needs, often to the detriment of their future (Debats 1996; Newcomb & Harlow 1986). To relax, they might withdraw effort rather than pursue their interests. To alleviate unease, they might abuse various substances or vent their anger. To override concerns with money, they might gamble irresponsibly.

As meaning diminishes, individuals thus act impulsively and irresponsibly. They will not embrace the challenges and complications – the uncertainty, anxiety and unease – that learning and development entails. They will not feel robust or resilient (Britt, Adler & Bartone 2001).

At the same time as their resilience diminishes, their relationships also decline. Without meaning, individuals strive to fulfill their immediate needs: they do not sacrifice their interests now to consolidate their relationships in the future. They seem uncompromising and aloof – not warm or caring. Their friendships are epitomized by mistrust. Their romances are unfulfilling.

Chain stores and chain smoking

Some individuals assume that meaning and purpose is innate or entrenched, like blue eyes or narrow hips. They presume that some people are inherently purposeful and responsible as well as resilient and kind. Other people, they assume, are naturally impulsive, irresponsible and inconsiderate.

Research, however, indicates that purpose rather than impulsivity is not innate or entrenched. Informative studies into fast food, for example, have demonstrated that impulsivity can be modified.

One of the advertising slogans at KFC was 'Finger lickin' good'. This phrase was used, partly because the slogan 'We ruin your health and wellbeing just as effectively as McDonalds and Burger King' was considered too long. This observation is not intended as a criticism of the food: after all, in most chains, a healthier alternative is usually available. Instead, the problem with these outlets – a problem that is not entirely the fault of the companies themselves – is far more profound.

Specifically, as some disquieting studies have shown, even exposure to icons that symbolize these chains affects the behaviour of people. When people observe the golden arches of McDonalds or the image of Colonel Sanders, for example, they tend to become more impulsive and impetuous. These individuals initiate actions that fulfill their immediate needs, often to the detriment of future goals. For example, as studies show, when people are exposed to icons, they are more likely to squander or to gamble their money, recklessly and irresponsibly (Zhong & DeVoe 2010).

This pattern of behaviour emanates from the associations that individuals form between fast food and indulgence. In general, when people feel the motivation to indulge – to satisfy their immediate urges rather than pursue their future goals – they are more inclined to visit one of these outlets. Over time, they form an association between these ubiquitous outlets and decadent motivations. When individuals drive past one of these chains, unconscious memories of utter indulgence are thus evoked. These memories then shape the behaviour of individuals, provoking these impulsive inclinations.

If iconic symbols of fast food can provoke impetuous behaviour, surely features of workplaces – features that impinge on employees throughout the day – should also shape their level of purpose instead of impulsivity. The question then becomes one of which characteristics of organizations foster meaning and purpose in employees and managers. Which characteristics of organizations will enhance the lives of individuals?

To foster this sense of meaning, organizations need only cultivate four conditions: cooperation, control, coherence, and contribution (for similar taxonomies, see Baumeister 1991; Heine, Proulx & Vohs 2006). When these four conditions are fulfilled, individuals will, almost inevitably, experience this feeling of purpose.

Condition 1: A cooperative environment

The first condition is cooperation. Individuals need to feel that people, in general, are cooperative and supportive. They need to believe that people are trustworthy – that people will follow social conventions and reciprocate favors.

If people are not cooperative – e.g. if they violate social conventions – many unforeseen complications can unfold. Specifically, individuals might be exploited or harmed. The facets of their life that they cherish, such as their health and reputation, might be threatened. When these problems are imminent, individuals cannot shift their attention to the future. They cannot reflect upon their future purpose.

Many studies have shown that uncooperative environments in which individuals feel excluded rather than trusted evoke feelings of futility instead of meaning. To illustrate, in one study university students were instructed to describe themselves on video. Other people, supposedly, watched the video to decide whether or not they would like to meet these students. Hours later, some students were informed they had been rejected by all the viewers. These students were not only offended, but also became more likely to perceive their life as devoid of meaning and purpose (Stillman *et al.* 2009).

Unfortunately, the culture and climate of many organizations is competitive rather than cooperative. Employees are encouraged to outperform, rather than support, rival companies as well as each other. Only the individuals who exceed targets – e.g. who attract more clients or sell more products than everyone else – are offered positions of prestige and privilege. Only the individuals who thrive are guaranteed job security.

Indeed, competition has escalated and cooperation has plummeted over recent decades. Many employees, in a raft of professions ranging from accountants to medical practitioners, perceive their workplace more competitive now than in previous decades (e.g. Bell & Fay 1997).

Admittedly, to compensate many organizations attempt to introduce initiatives, programs or policies intended to foster cooperation. They might, for example, impose display rules – regulations on how employees should behave as they interact with customers, colleagues, managers or other individuals. Employees are directed to seem friendly and amicable rather than frustrated, curt, angry or uneasy.

These attempts might, at least initially, enhance cooperation. However, these practices compromise the other conditions that facilitate meaning. To illustrate, when display rules are imposed and employees are told to seem content and friendly, their behaviour actually becomes more erratic. They strive to suppress their frustrations, irritations and other unacceptable states.

These attempts, however, are exhausting. They deplete energy and promote burnout (Grandey 2003). As their mental energy subsides, the capacity of these individuals to suppress their frustrations dissipates. They often explode in anger, unexpectedly and needlessly.

In addition, as their motivation diminishes they are not as likely to behave responsibly. They refrain from tedious activities such as safety practices. They are, as research shows, more likely to be the victims of accidents at work (Nahrgang, Morgeson and Hofmann 2011).

Display rules, therefore, are intended to cultivate a cohesive and supportive environment. However, when these policies are introduced, individuals cannot as readily control or regulate their behaviour as effectively. They cannot prevent adversities as effectively. They cannot, therefore, fulfill the second key determinant of meaning: control.

Condition 2: A sense of control

The second condition, essential to meaning, is a sense of control. Specifically, individuals do not only need to feel that other people will observe the norms, standards and expectations of the environment. They also need to feel they can fulfill these norms themselves. They need to feel that they will not violate the standards and expectations of other people.

If people do not feel they can fulfill these standards, they anticipate imminent problems. They feel they may be punished or harmed imminently. They cannot, therefore, shift their attention to their future purpose.

The prevailing trends in modern organizations have compromised this sense of control. Apart from display rules, other initiatives intended to promote cooperation and collaboration have compromised this sense of control.

Specifically, major decisions have become increasingly centralized. Most of the key changes in organizations – the termination of a business unit, transformation in the measures of performance, or the introduction of a strategic plan – are decided unilaterally, usually by a small cell of senior managers. These changes are communicated to employees later, sometimes after the transformations have been initiated, with limited if any consultation or discussion (Sennett 2006).

Supposedly, as many executives maintain, major decisions need to be centralized. In the sprawling and dynamic organizations of today, few employees, at least in large companies, understand all the complexities and constraints that need to be accommodated. Few employees could offer valid insights. If decisions were not centralized, each workgroup or department would operate in isolation of each other, impeding collaboration and undermining cooperation.

Nevertheless, when authority is confined to a cadre of executives, employees do not feel a sense of control. They often feel that some unforeseen change, and thus unanticipated complications, could unfold at any moment.

In one consulting firm, an employee was reprimanded after instinctively shaking hands with a manager. Specifically, to safeguard senior personnel from needless germs, this greeting between employees and managers had been prohibited the year before.

Furthermore, authorities do not always justify their decisions to employees unambiguously. Employees are not, therefore, always certain of the precise objectives, preferences and expectations of managers. They are not certain of their rights or responsibilities. Because of this uncertainty, they do not feel they can demonstrate initiative, concerned their choices or decisions might contradict the preferences and expectations of managers (Sigler & Pearson 2000). They do not feel they are granted any autonomy or independence – i.e. any opportunity to utilize their own judgment or insight.

As the autonomy of many employees dissipates, the organization becomes increasingly hierarchical. Senior managers are bestowed almost unmitigated power, influence and ultimately privilege. Middle managers understand the primary motivations of key decisions and therefore occasionally feel that they can reach their own decisions, but within strict boundaries. Other employees, however, are granted considerably fewer opportunities to demonstrate initiative and to control their environment. They feel increasingly exposed to the unpredictable whims of other people.

Once the organization becomes hierarchical, the decisions become increasingly unjust. Even when their intentions are pure, managers tend to underestimate the anxiety and apprehension that employees experience. They tend to dismiss these concerns.

As one study showed, when managers are granted positions of privilege they even dismiss the intolerable anguish that inexorable bullying can evoke. If individuals are immune to this harassment, they underestimate the intensity of these feelings. As soon as they are bullied or harassed themselves, even in the context of a simulation, their perceptions change dramatically (Nordgren, Banas & MacDonald 2010). They immediately introduce policies that protect employees from belligerent colleagues or aggressive managers.

Eventually, as stress leave mounts, employees depart and conflict escalates, organizations will institute policies that are intended to instill a sense of control. For example, some organizations will institute policies that, supposedly, demonstrate the benevolence and support of the organization and management. They will, for example, disseminate documents that stipulate the values of this organization – values like compassion, integrity and community. They will introduce policies or provision that, supposedly, enhance the wellbeing of employees. Employees are granted the option to work at home, suspend their career, discuss their problems with a counselor, and many other benefits.

However, after organizations introduce provisions that are intended to support the wellbeing of employees, several complications prevail. Employees feel motivated to utilize these benefits, perhaps working from home. However, they also feel compelled to abstain from these provisions as well. If they work at home, suspend their career or consider the other provisions, they suspect their opportunities might wane or their reputation might decline in the future. They experience conflicting motives, compromising their motivation.

Indeed, as research has shown, when organizations introduce policies that supposedly balance work and family life, employees do not become more committed and loyal to the workplace. Their commitment actually tends to dissipate, especially if the leaders are not particularly effective (Wang & Walumbwa 2007).

Indeed, many initiatives introduced to decrease the vulnerability of employees and instill a sense of control actually elicit competing goals and conflicting desires. These contradictions then impede the third condition that fosters meaning: coherence.

Condition 3: Coherent standards & expectations

The third source of meaning and purpose is coherence. Individuals need to feel the expectations of managers are consistent over time. They need to believe the standards of this organization and the goals they need to pursue are compatible with each other. Without this consistency, individuals cannot be certain which activities will be rewarded in the future. Without this coherence, individuals cannot be sure their aspirations and purpose will be rewarding or fulfilling in the future.

Over recent decades, the expectations of managers and the standards of organizations have become increasingly incompatible with one another. For example, many organizations have introduced an arrangement, called a matrix structure, in which every workgroup or department is managed by two people: one person is an expert in the industry and the other person is an expert in the field. Therefore, each employee must fulfill the expectations of two managers.

In some instances, these managers impose contradictory expectations. One manager, perhaps with expertise in the education industry, might want employees to recommend ambitious alternatives. The other manager, perhaps with expertise in accounting, might want employees to recommend more prudent and economical alternatives.

Consequently, employees are subjected to contradictory demands. They are not certain which standards to fulfill and which goals to pursue.

Other recent trends in many organizations exacerbate this conflict. To illustrate, in recent decades the workload of employees and managers has soared. In 2002, dual earners in the US tended to work approximately 90 hours a week (Bond *et al.* 2003). Only three decades earlier, this figure was only 80 hours a week.

Because workloads has escalated, employees and managers are granted no time or opportunity to debate the standards, objectives and values of the organization. They cannot debate, for example, the benefits and drawbacks of their prescribed values, e.g. honesty, service and responsibility. They need to orient their attention to immediate demands rather than abstract principles.

Yet, such debate has been shown to curb the contradictions that pervade organizations. Without this debate, managers tend to vary their values over time. When the demands are manageable rather than excessive, managers are more likely to embrace the prescribed values of the work environment. If the values of this organization are honesty, service and responsibility, they are more likely to reward sincere, cooperative and dependable employees. When the demands mount, however, managers tend to dismiss these values. They prefer employees to sacrifice their values and merely fulfill the deadlines.

However, as research shows, when managers are granted opportunities to debate these values, this inconsistency subsides. Managers are more likely to maintain their values, even during more demanding times (Maio *et al.* 2001).

Actually, many of the practices that organizations introduce to clarify the standards, expectations and preferences of managers – and to stipulate which behaviours and qualities will be rewarded – provoke other complications. For example, many organizations attempt to stipulate the precise expectations of every employee.

If employees are classified as Code 153, for example, they must write five reports, attend two meetings, coordinate one project and participate in one workshop to receive their bonus. These tangible criteria are assumed to override imprecision and to clarify expectations. These objective imperatives are presumed to overcome the problems of subjective, and thus biased, judgments.

For example, if managers apply these objective criteria, they often inhibit initiative. Employees do not enact behaviours they feel are helpful but not prescribed. Indeed, these precise objectives have even been shown to increase the incidence of theft (Levine & Jackson 2002).

Furthermore, in these environments employees merely strive to fulfill their duties rather than pursue their aspirations. Consequently, their primary motivation is to minimize errors (Friedman & Forster 2001).

Admittedly, in some circumstances, error scan be devastating. In one American company, all the managers received an email entitled 'Share information for job applicants'. The email reported that some job applicants had received misleading information about the employee share scheme – an issue that was soon to be investigated by a corporate regulator. Unfortunately, one manager misconstrued the title and distributed the email to ongoing job applicants.

Although blunders can be consequential, a culture in which employees are afraid to commit any errors can impede development. When individuals strive to prevent mistakes, however, their learning is stifled. They do not acquire skills and insights as readily.

For example, in one study, while learning a software program, some participants were encouraged to press the wrong buttons occasionally. Other participants were instructed to abstain from these errors. If participants had been invited to commit errors, their subsequent performance on this software was especially proficient (Heimbeck *et al.* 2003). These individuals were more inclined to experiment with various alternatives and possibilities.

Over time, these individuals begin to feel they cannot develop their expertise and competence (Dweck 2006). They do not perceive feedback and criticism as an opportunity to learn and, therefore, often seem defensive. They do not feel they can cultivate a distinct and valuable collection of skills and abilities, impeding the final determinant of purpose and meaning: contribution.

Condition 4: A distinct contribution

The final source of purpose and meaning is contribution. Individuals do not only need to understand which pursuits or achievements are rewarded, they need to feel they can they can offer a distinct contribution to accomplish one of these objectives.

If they cannot offer a distinct contribution – if their qualities are not in demand – they know their attempts will not be rewarded. They know their endeavors will be unfulfilling. Their sense of inspiration and direction thus dissipates.

In modern organizations, however, individuals seldom feel distinct. Nowadays, in response to trivial changes in the market or industry, organizations often transform their activities and operations. They will often introduce a department or program to exploit some recent opportunity. They will often abandon an ongoing project because of waning demand. Employees, therefore, often need to adjust rapidly, assuming a role they have never filled before. They have to learn tasks they have not attempted previously.

Organizations, therefore, tend to seek employees who can adapt promptly (Sennett 2006). They are not as motivated to attract employees who have developed a distinct and advanced skill. They feel these skills might be obsolete in the future. Employees, therefore, are seldom granted opportunities to cultivate and hone their skills and qualities. They do not feel they can offer a unique contribution.

The solution

Organizations, therefore, introduce a variety of initiatives intended to fulfill the determinants of meaning: cooperation, control, coherence and contribution. Initiatives that enhance one source of meaning, however, tend to compromise another source of meaning.

Fortunately, some programs, policies and projects do not elicit these problems. These initiatives enhance one, or even more, sources of meaning without significantly impeding the other sources. This book identifies the programs or policies that fulfill this objective and, therefore, satisfy the genuine needs of most employees.

Admittedly, not everyone will seek the same workplace characteristics. Some people will apply to work at more competitive, spirited or even ruthless companies. Other people, in contrast, may seek more communal, charitable or benevolent organizations. Likewise, some people might apply to work at an innovative, creative firm, whereas other people might gravitate towards more traditional, conservative workplaces.

Therefore, at first glance you might assume that no particular cluster of workplace characteristics can be regarded as preferable. No organization will satisfy every employee.

Nevertheless, satisfaction at work does not always translate into meaning and wellbeing. For example, in some environments job satisfaction can impede creativity, a key facet of wellbeing and development (Zhou & George 2001). An organization that encourages competitive, even duplicitous, behaviour might satisfy some employees but will tend to compromise purpose and progress. A dynamic and unpredictable environment can promote job satisfaction but will usually curtail meaning.

Therefore, the workplace characteristics that increase job satisfaction, and attract employees, do not always foster meaning and purpose. Although the features of organizations that evoke satisfaction might vary across individuals, the features that promote meaning and wellbeing – cooperation, control, coherence and contribution – do not vary as appreciably.

Part B

The Physical Surroundings

Chapter 4

Objects and artefacts

On the website of this company are several photographs of the workplace. The photographs are obviously contrived to ensure that everyone seems happy and enthusiastic. But, your attention is instead directed to the objects and artefacts in the room: the pictures, lamps, equipment, and furniture. For example, several prints, each of a different person, are dispersed across a wall. Most of these people are children, playing happily. Other people are teenagers, with a more rebellious demeanour. The light bulbs on every lamp are naked, devoid of a shade. However, this style was not intended to save money. The other objects and furniture are luxurious and expensive. The rounded, designer chairs and tables, the stylish round tables and many other pieces seem lavish and elegant. The computers are a mixture of PCs and Macs. These features are heartening, apart from one concern...

The objects and artefacts in most entrances and offices are often intended to shape the image and reputation of organizations. Chic and fashionable ornaments and furnishings are supposed to show that the company is popular and trendy. Grand and opulent furniture is intended to demonstrate that the organization is prosperous and successful. An informed observer, however, can uncover information about the organization that managers had not intended to convey.

Works of art

The paintings and prints that decorate the walls often reflect, and even exacerbate, some of the problems and challenges that pervade the organization. Research, for example, shows the personality of individuals shapes their art preferences (Furnham & Walker 2001). If individuals prefer realistic paintings to abstract art, they are more likely to be conservative, methodical, disciplined and conscientious. Nevertheless, if they like pop art – a movement that is often characterized by aggressive images – they are more likely to be brusque, abrupt, disagreeable and unsympathetic. Therefore, the art that permeates the environment sometimes manifests the preferences, and hence the personality, of the most influential managers in the organization

The art does not only reflect, but also affects, the behaviour, attitude and personality of managers and employees in the organization. For example, in particular conditions, when individuals are exposed to photographs of a library, they behaviour changes. They become more inclined, for example, to speak quietly (Aarts & Dijkersterhuis 2003).

Furthermore, this inclination to speak quietly can then even shape their mood. That is, after individuals assume this quiet, reserved and subdued demeanour, they feel more introverted. This feeling of introversion then evokes a mild sense of dejection or melancholy, curbing their excitement and animation (McNiel & Fleeson 2006).

The paintings and prints that decorate the walls, therefore, represent a telling source of important information about the work environment. Research has indeed demonstrated that paintings affect the likelihood that people cherish conformity rather than creativity. In one study, some participants were exposed to photographs of people in suits, probably accountants, representing a conservative occupation. Other participants were exposed to photographs of punks, representing deviation from conservative standards.

Next, a series of 100 or so beeps was emitted in a room. All participants completed a task in which they needed to estimate the number of beeps that were presented over a speaker. These participants first heard the answers of other people. These people, unbeknownst to participants, were actually actors. These people deliberately overestimated the number of beeps. They suggested answers like 120, 130 or 140, knowing the actual number of beats was really 100. Finally, the participants then presented their response.

If participants had been exposed to photographs of accountants, instead of punks, they tended to conform to the other answers. That is, if everyone else maintained that 120 to 140 beeps were presented, the participants agreed. These individuals, therefore, valued conformity over creativity (Pendry & Carrick 2001).

Therefore, if the prints or paintings in this organization depict compliant or conservative individuals, perhaps dressed in suits or uniforms, managers are likely to value conformity. They will often expect employees to respect the traditions of the workplace. They believe the established practices must be followed; deviations are not tolerated.

At first glance, this conformity does not seem objectionable. However, in many instances, when traditions are revered, obsolete practices cannot be forcefully questioned. Regulations or procedures that impede progress and compromise satisfaction cannot be relaxed. Intractable problems cannot be addressed efficiently. Novel, original and creative solutions are rejected, even derived, rather than considered and implemented.

In one organization in the UK, two conservative managers were discussing how to occupy their teenage children during the holidays. Overhearing their discussion, one employee suggested 'Grand Theft Auto'. Unaware that he was referring to a computer game, he was dismissed the next day.

Indeed, this aversion to creativity pervades many organizations. In one study, for example, professional recruiters evaluated the resumes of job candidates. The design of some resumes was creative. The information was presented in circles or squares, arranged in an artistic pattern. The design of other resumes was plain and traditional.

When the qualifications and experiences of two job candidates were the same, the recruiters chose the person who submitted a plain design instead of a creative design (Arnulf, Tegner & Larssen 2010). Originality is often regarded with suspicion. Tradition is frequently preferred.

When creativity is disparaged, not only do problems often persist, but the mood of employees is also compromised. That is, when individuals become absorbed in more creative tasks, their mood is often lifted. They feel more enthused and cheerful. When creativity is deterred, however, individuals are more likely to feel dull and uninspired (Hirt, Devers & McCrea 2008).

> **✗** In some organizations, the pictures or prints in the surroundings tend to depict compliant or conservative individuals, perhaps dressed in suits or uniforms. In these organizations, conformity rather than creativity is embraced. Employees who diverge from the customs and traditions of this organization tend to be criticised or derogated. In these environments, you might not feel that your distinct contributions will be valued and appreciated.

In the dark

Even the attire of managers and employees can amplify this aversion to creativity. In many professional organizations, all the managers, and most of the employees, wear dark, formal suits. Not only do suits provoke conformity, the dark colour actually exacerbates the problem. That is, when exposed to a vast sea of dark clothes, managers and employees are even more inclined to conform. Creativity and originality is even more likely to be eschewed.

For instance, in one study participants read brief extracts of court transcripts. Their task was to decide whether the perpetrators were guilty. Four other people, actually confederates of the researcher, also pretended to complete the same task. That is, these four other people read the material and offered an opinion on whether the perpetrators were guilty.

Sometimes, the participants conformed to the opinions of these four people. That is, if the four people all maintained the perpetrators were guilty, the participants expressed the same opinion. If the four people all maintained the perpetrators were innocent, the participants agreed. On other occasions, the participants did not conform to the opinions of these four people.

Interestingly, the clothes these four people wore influenced whether or not participants would conform (Vrij, Pannell & Ost 2005). If the four people donned dark clothes, participants tended to conform. That is, they expressed the same opinion as the four confederates. If the four people donned clothes that were light in colour, participants expressed their own opinions. They were willing to diverge.

Therefore, when managers wear dark clothes, employees are often reluctant to express their opinions or think creatively. Instead, they feel stifled. Specifically, although unconscious, people associate darkness with menace. The environment feels more ominous and threatening. They will, therefore, feel pressure to conform, and they will not feel secure enough to challenge the traditions and practices of the organization.

> ✓ On the website or other documentation, you might be able to locate photographs of managers in the workplace. Sometimes, many of the managers don relatively casual attire, often with lighter colours. In these organizations, creativity is embraced. You will probably feel that your distinct contributions are cherished and that unexpected criticism is unlikely.

A picture of innocence

In addition to conformity, the art, décor and attire can also affect the extent to which managers and employees are supportive, cooperative and collaborative. To illustrate, some paintings depict a particular constituency – perhaps elderly citizens, children, surfers or footballers. When individuals observe these paintings, they become more inclined to enact the behaviours they usually undertake when they interact with this constituency (Cesario, Plaks & Higgins 2006). If the picture depicts elderly citizens, individuals tend to walk more slowly and express more conservative opinions. If children appear in these pictures, individuals are more inclined to act compassionately and supportively.

In general, when individuals interact with a child or some other innocent, but dependent, person or community, they tend to act more cooperatively. They might show compassion or offer assistance, for example. Thus, if an organization is teeming with paintings of these dependent constituencies or communities, the managers are more likely to behave supportively as well. The culture is usually more collaborative instead of competitive

To illustrate, in one organization, in Brazil, a few prints depicting children were displayed on the walls. One day, an employee, obviously upset, arrived late to work despite living only two blocks away. Her kind supervisor, sensing her distress, asked her what had happened. With a forlorn tone, she told him that her dog had fled during the morning and had not been found. The manager decided to assemble as many employees as possible – over half the organization, including the leadership team – to scour the streets and locate the dog. The dog was eventually found, over fours later, unharmed but relieved to see his owner.

Some works of art promote dedication and achievement. In one study, some participants were exposed to a picture of a woman prevailing in a foot race. None of the other contestants appeared in the shot. Other participants were not exposed to this picture.

Next, participants completed a work task. Their task was to attract donations to a cause. If participants had earlier been exposed to the triumphant runner, they tended to attract more donations from benefactors.

Nevertheless, the pursuit of achievement can sometimes, but not always, escalate into undesirable motivations. Individuals might develop a competitive mindset, sometimes manifesting as hostile, duplicitous or aggressive behaviour. Alternatively, individuals might become fixated on achievement, neglecting more cooperative and communal needs such as their family and friends. To prevent these complications, images of achievement should be coupled with depictions of cooperation.

> ✔ Occasionally, the pictures or prints in the surroundings tend to depict somewhat dependent people or communities, such as children. In these organizations, managers tend to be more cooperative and supportive.

A light bulb moment

Cartoons are a veritable source of vital information. Without cartoons, for example, most people would overestimate the intelligence of coyotes: although Acme products are invariably defective, coyotes will remain obsessively loyal to this brand.

Perhaps a more important insight, however, also illustrated by cartoons, is that light bulbs generate important solutions. That is, after a light bulb appears in the thought bubble of cartoon characters, the protagonists almost inevitably have a great idea.

This association between an illuminated light bulb and insightful solutions now pervades our culture. Indeed, because of this association, some exciting studies have recently shown that light bulbs, when illuminated, actually enhance insight.

In one study, participants received a series of questions. An example is: 'If four dots are arranged in the shape of a square, how can you connect all these dots with only three straight lines?' Another example is: 'What is the word that is associated with mill, tooth, and dust?'

While they completed these questions, some participants sat near a naked light bulb that had been illuminated. Other participants sat near a light bulb that had been obscured by a lampshade but was nevertheless illuminated. If the participants sat near a visible, illuminated light bulb, they were more likely to answer the questions correctly (Slepian *et al.* 2010). The association they formed between light bulbs and insightful solutions might have somehow boosted their confidence or enhanced their thinking.

Therefore, if several naked, visible light bulbs are illuminated in the workplace, the employees will tend to be more insightful. Recurring problems will often be solved, and the environment is likely to be productive.

> ✓ In a limited proportion of work environments, some of the light bulbs are visible – rather than obscured by lampshades – as well as illuminated. In these environments, you might feel your solutions and suggestions are more insightful. You may, therefore, feel your contributions are constructive.

Brand new

The design, fixtures and furnishings of some companies seem particularly original and creative. The reception of one law firm in Sydney, for example, is teeming with unusual objects, like a huge log, a miniature Ferris wheel and an inclined ladder that does not lead anywhere. The director of this company, presumably, is either a creative person or a giant rat.

Although not as unusual, creative features often permeate other organizations as well. The foyer might resemble a beach, with towels on the ground, a beach lounge in the corner, and even an ice cream van near a wall. Alternatively, the originality might be more subtle. Perhaps a small cage with a few lizards might be located near the entrance.

Creative features tend to affect the behaviour of employees. When individuals are exposed to creative features, their creativity actually improves. Their solutions, therefore, are often more original and effective, and problems are not as persistent

Furthermore, when managers embrace creativity, they cherish exploration over perfection. They accept errors and risks. They are not as concerned when mistakes are committed. Employees, therefore, do not feel as anxious or worried. They feel like they are granted the license to explore ideas and to propose suggestions, stimulating growth and progress.

Research does indeed show that creative features improve creative ability. Even brand names that people associate with creativity and originality have been shown to enhance these capabilities.

In one study, for example, participants observed some words on a computer screen. Occasionally, a brand name appeared fleetingly – too briefly to be recognized consciously. In particular, some participants were exposed to the brand name 'Apple'. Other participants were exposed to the brand name 'IBM'. Although both companies are actually remarkably innovative, people tend to associate Apple, and not IBM, with creativity and originality.

Next, participants completed a task that assessed creativity. They were instructed to identify as many creative uses as possible for a brick. For example, a brick could be attached to the bottom of a shoe, beneficial if one leg is longer than the other. Alternatively, a brick could be gift wrapped and sent as a present.

If participants had been subliminally exposed to the brand name Apple instead of IBM, they offered more creative answers to this question (Fitzsimons, Chartrand & Fitzsimons 2008). Exposure to names, objects or other features that epitomize creativity tend to elicit a more innovative and receptive approach.

> ✓ Creative and novel features – that is, features that diverge from traditional offices – permeate some work environments. Alternatively, some of the brands in these offices epitomize creativity, such as at least one Mac computer. In these offices, you are likely to feel that your distinct contributions are cherished. Managers are also unlikely to criticize errors or shortfalls unfairly. The environment is more predictable, and you are likely to experience a sense of control.

A wealth of envy

Rather than depict themselves as creative and innovative, many organizations attempt to impress customers, as well as other stakeholders, with their opulent surroundings. The entrance is often magnificent, with luxurious furnishings and immaculate decor. The view may be imposing, and the furniture might be exclusive.

Such lavish surroundings, however, provoke a range of problems. First, when school children arrive requesting donations to purchase a box of cookies, the usual response of: 'I'm sorry, but we're a bit tight this month' is not quite as compelling as usual. But, perhaps more importantly, lavish surroundings often incite fraudulent behaviour.

To illustrate, as some illuminating research shows, after individuals observe affluence, they unsurprisingly experience envy. In the aftermath of this envy, individuals feel compelled to redress inequalities. In essence, they feel entitled to behave deceptively, or even illegally, to increase their earnings. In one study, for example, after participants observed thousands of dollars piled on a desk, they were subsequently more likely to cheat on a subsequent test (Gino & Pierce 2009).

Similarly, in one law firm in Japan, a manager noticed that one of his missing pens, an expensive Mont Blank, was sitting conspicuously on the desk of an employee. The employee insisted that he had bought the pen himself. The manager then showed the inscription to the employee and asked: 'Then why has my wife written you a loving message?'

This duplicitous behaviour can undermine the cohesion of workgroups. For example, some employees might exaggerate their contributions to some project, or even pinch ideas from someone else. Other individuals will eventually begin to realize that some people have behaved manipulatively. Trust will plummet. A competitive, rather than cooperative, environment will eventually prevail.

For example, in one printing company, located in a lavish building, one male supervisor was supposed to scrutinize the reports written by his three female employees. Rather than analyze these reports carefully, he would simply remove the name of these individuals and claim authorship himself. Administrative staff would then dispatch the report to the designated client.

One day, however, one of the employees decided to submit a personal story to the company newsletter – a newsletter that often published biographical accounts of interesting employees. The supervisor erroneously assumed the story was a report, and claimed authorship again. The company were very surprised to discover that the male supervisor had the previous month undergone a traumatic hysterectomy.

Rather than dedicate exorbitant sums to purchase lavish fittings, some organizations instead infuse the environment with imitation furnishings. The rugs, tiles, chairs, tables, ornaments and other items are all inexpensive replicas. This alternative might curb expenses, but it does not improve morality. Actually, exposure to imitations has been shown to provoke more deception. In one study, conducted by Gino, Norton, and Ariel (2010), participants wore either genuine or counterfeit sunglasses. Participants who wore the counterfeit items were more likely to cheat on a subsequent test.

Exposure to these items, conceivably, activates the memory or awareness that people are often contrived, and as a result insincerity frequently permeates the environment. Thus, dishonest and duplicitous behaviour is perceived as common and, consequently, acceptable.

> ✗ In many workplaces, especially in large corporations, the fittings or surroundings in the office seem particularly opulent, extravagant or lavish in style. In these workplaces, trust between colleagues and managers – as well as between employees – is often limited. The culture is competitive and not collaborative.

Edgy furniture

Even the shapeof furnishings and fittings, instead of merely the expense, may be informative. Some revealing studies have shown that cooperative, supportive managers are more inclined to prefer curved shapes (Zhang, Feick & Price 2006). They might, for example, gravitate towards round tables rather than rectangular tables. They might also like couches with a curved back or rounded cushions

In contrast, more competitive managers – managers who are sometimes confrontational or even aggressive – are more inclined to prefer angular shapes. They like furnishings and ornaments, including benches, tables, couches and artwork, with straight edges and boxlike designs.

Obviously, the managers themselves do not usually design the office. However, if most of the managers are confrontational, and thus prefer angular shapes, they will tend to choose offices that align to these preferences. When they seek an office, they will, often unconsciously, feel repelled by curved designs. Similarly, if these managers need to decide whether to extend their existing lease, they are also more likely to leave whenever the design does not match their preferences. In short, the design of an office does sometimes reflect the personality of managers.

✓ Frequently, the furnishings, fittings and design of the workspace seems to be more curved than angular. Many of the edges are rounded instead of straight. In these workplaces, managers are more likely to be cooperative than confrontational.

Chapter 5

Design and layout

As you walk into the lobby, you peer into your mobile telephone, pretending to read an important message. While nobody is watching, you attempt to survey the work environment, just behind the glass doors. You observe an expansive office. Scattered around the office are many smaller rooms. The walls are painted white, with a hint of red. The smaller rooms are surrounded by generous windows. The work environment is illuminated with radiant, natural light. Situated outside the windows is a peaceful courtyard. A subtle trace of citrus pervades the air. You feel encouraged by this scene, apart from one concern...

The design and layout of an office space is a key source of valuable information, at least to the trained observer. Occasionally, this workspace can be observed from the outside or from the reception area. In other instances, the workspace may appear on the website. Finally, in some organizations the work environment is concealed from the public but can perhaps be observed during or after the interview.

Seeing red

The prevailing colour of the work environment – particularly the walls – is a vital source of important information. In general, when the surroundings are primarily light blue or green, employees and managers are not quite as likely to be irritable or disagreeable. They are, instead, more likely to seem unhurried, patient, tolerant and accommodating. Feelings of anxiety and disquiet tend to abate.

In one study, participants had to wait while downloading some photographs of houses and rooms from the internet. The computer stalled for 17.5 seconds. During this time, the screen was either light blue or light yellow. Later, participants needed to specify the extent to which they felt the photographs were downloaded quickly or slowly.

If the screen was light blue, participants seemed patient and unperturbed. They felt the material was downloaded quickly. If the screen was yellow, in contrast, participants were more impatient and irritable (Gorn *et al.* 2004).

> ✔ If the main colour that pervades the work environment is light green or light blue, individuals in the workplace will tend to be patient instead of irritable. You might experience a sense of control and predictability.

Red walls and items, in contrast, can provoke various problems in the organizations. Specifically at school, and later at work, individuals learn to associate red with failure. Teachers and managers, for example, often use read pen to indicate errors. Dangers signs, stop signals and other reproachful messages usually appear in red letters. Phrases or expressions that connote a problem or shortfall also often entail the word red: 'see red', 'be in the red', 'red tape', 'like a red rag to a bull', 'catch red-handed', 'code red', 'red flag', 'red light district', and 'red herring'.

Because of these associations, when individuals are exposed to red surroundings or items, particularly at work, their primary motivation is to avert failure. They feel a profound urge to prevent criticism. They become especially worried they might commit an error or disappoint an authority. They feel compelled to fulfil, rather than breach, the prevailing standards and expectations of managers. They strive to satisfy their immediate duties and neglect future aspirations. They orient their attention to errors instead of opportunities, to problems instead of progress.

Scientific investigations have confirmed this possibility that red directs attention to error. When teachers correct work with a red pen, instead of a blue pen, for example, they identify more errors (Rutchick, Slepian & Ferris 2010), and the grades they award tend to be harsher.

This inclination of employees and managers to orient their attention to problems and obstacles rather than to opportunities and aspirations can initiate several complications. First, the employees do not feel they are granted the support to cultivate their qualities. In these environments, employees feel that they must not commit any errors, and that they need to avoid mistakes.

These individuals, therefore, will be reluctant to experiment with unfamiliar tasks. They will not attempt to operate a machine, utilize software, or undertake a project they have never attempted before. They will not embrace the risks and uncertainty that progress entails. They feel stagnant; they do not acquire pertinent skills.

Second, in these environments employees are inclined to worry and fret incessantly. That is, when managers direct their attention to errors, employees are often castigated – usually unexpectedly. The employees, therefore, anticipate these tirades. They experience an unrelenting sense of uncertainty and unpredictability, distracting their concentration. In one large telecommunications company, an employee was castigated because she misplaced a comma.

Scientific experiments have confirmed this possibility. In one example, participants were exposed to the word red or blue, inserted discretely at the bottom of a page. The word red was sufficient to impair the capacity of these individuals to solve logical puzzles (Lichtenfeld *et al.* 2009).

✘ If red pens are visible – or if some of the signs appear in red letters – you might not be as likely to develop your skills; you may instead experience a sense of apprehension, concerned you will commit errors. You are not as likely to feel your contributions are distinct or the environment predictable.

Open-plan offices and close-minded individuals

In modern societies, open-plan offices are common, even ubiquitous. Employees are seldom assigned their own office. They are even seldom assigned an office with only one or two other people. Instead, they usually work in an office with 30, 40 or more people, separated only by flimsy partitions.

Admittedly, some people work reasonably well in these environments. As research indicates, extraverted, sociable, confident and gregarious people actually work more effectively when other people are nearby (Uziel 2007). They feel energized and inspired by other people. They may work as well, if not better, in open-plan offices than in traditional offices. More introverted, reserved and reflective people, however, do not work as well when other people are nearby. They are not suited to open-plan offices.

Regardless, in general, open-plan offices tend to reduce trust. That is, to establish trust, individuals first need to feel secure. They need to feel they can return to a protected and private space whenever necessary, which is sometimes called a safe haven. They need to feel they can flee complications.

Without this provision, individuals shun risks. They strive to prevent problems. Therefore, to curb these risks, they remain detached from other people. They do not want to become too close, concerned they might be rejected. They become reluctant to form close relationships or to collaborate effectively.

Research has vindicated this concern. In open-plan offices, employees are not as likely to form established, trusting and cooperative relationships with colleagues and managers (Brennan, Chugh & Kline 2002). The environment is not as cooperative and collaborative.

> ✓ In some organizations, the office does not conform to an open-plan design. Employees are granted their own office, or share with one or two people. Alternatively, employees are granted the right to use a private office at short notice. In these organizations, the environment is more cooperative and conflicts are uncommon.

Let there be light

Many workplaces are saturated with natural light. Most of these employees are situated near a window. The windows are expansive, permitting the sun to penetrate the glass throughout most of the day.

Other workplaces are dim. Many employees are concealed in makeshift offices with no windows. Heavy blinds, curtains or shutters obscure the sun. The office seems to have been designed by vampires with sensitive skin.

Interestingly, when the workplace is dim, employees are more inclined to behave deceptively. Corrupt, illicit, improper and objectionable behaviours are common.

Although unconscious, employees tend to associate darkness with anonymity. They do not feel as accountable in these dim conditions. Although they might actually be entirely visible to managers, they feel anonymous and unaccountable.

Because individuals do not feel as accountable, they are more inclined to act inappropriately. They might disseminate false rumors, or withhold important information. Consequently, events that could have been predicted unfold unexpectedly. Unforeseen changes and unanticipated demands often transpire. The workplace seems unpredictable, and the employees often feel stressed.

Research has indeed confirmed that these are adverse consequences of dim conditions. In one experiment, some participants completed a task in a dim room. Other participants completed the same task in a room soaking in sunlight.

If the room was dim, participants were more inclined to cheat on this task. They were more inclined to exaggerate the number of answers they uncovered, for example. They were also more likely to act selfishly during another task, disregarding the needs and objectives of others. Even when participants merely donned sunglasses to obscure the light, they were still more inclined to behave duplicitously (Zhong, Bohns & Gino 2010).

* In some organizations, the work environment is dim. Windows are not visible from many offices. Alternatively, the windows are small or obscured with blinds. In these locations, unforeseen problems often unfold. Employees do not feel a sense of control.

Around the clock

Everyone of us, at least sometimes, feels lazy. We might allude to a vast array of tenuous excuses to justify our torpid behaviour. To postpone the arduous task of wheeling the bin to the curb, we might remind our spouse that the container is not yet bursting. Indeed, we might even swallow the core of an apple we just consumed. This act both guarantees that the bin is not full, and that we do not need to rise from the couch for another half hour.

On other occasions, however, we are energetic and spirited. To extract the final remnants of tomato sauce, we are willing to devote unbounded effort into the task of shaking the bottle vigorously and forcefully.

Unfortunately, if we work at a taxing and unfulfilling workplace, our capacity to mobilize this effort diminishes. Both at work as well as after we return home, we feel exhausted rather than animated. Our mental energy is depleted. Our capacity to devote the effort that is needed to develop skills, refine our practices and improve our performance subsides. Fortunately, several features of the work environment can replenish this energy and facilitate progress.

For example, if employees can readily observe a clock from their workspace, they can more readily sustain their effort over the day. That is, as research indicates, after individuals complete one taxing or demanding task, they often feel exhausted or drained. They are, therefore, not as inclined to monitor their performance or progress over the next few hours. Consequently, their effort and dedication tends to dissipate. Their capacity to complete another taxing or demanding task soon afterwards deteriorates.

Nevertheless, as scientists have shown, when a clock is nearby, this problem diminishes (Wan & Sternthal 2008). This clock prompts individuals to monitor their progress more vigilantly. These employees, therefore, are more inclined to sustain their effort and maintain their performance.

> ✓ In some organizations, clocks seem to be visible from most desks. In these organizations you are more likely to feel energetic and resolute, and to feel that you have contributed effectively.

Mother nature

More importantly, in some organizations images of nature pervades the environment. The building might be located in a verdant countryside or near the mountains. The offices might be surrounded by a courtyard teeming with plants. Alternatively, photographs of nature might appear on the walls or on screen savers.

Exposure to these images has been shown to replenish mental energy. After employees observe nature – either actual plants or merely photographed images – their capacity to complete tasks that demand concentration and effort improves. Their ability to maintain their effort, even after they complete taxing activities, is enhanced. Consequently, individuals are able to refine their skills and improve their abilities. They can undertake tasks that, initially, seem unnatural or unusual, a key determinant of learning and development.

Ten years ago, the managers of one advertising agency in New York distributed rockeries and ferneries, tastefully and inconspicuously, around the office. The ceiling was covered with the faint image of a canopy. Sounds of the forest, including gushing water and chirping birds, subtly permeated the atmosphere. Unfortunately, a few years later, the new CEO, who had recently been appointed, decided to deforest the environment. The skills of employees gradually diminished, and the level of innovation waned dramatically.

> ✓ In some offices or workspaces, employees can occasionally observe images of nature. In these environments, you are likely to feel energized enough to cultivate useful skills and distinct qualities, and to feel that you contribute effectively to the organization.

Smells like team spirit

Even the aroma that pervades an environment can affect the behaviour of employees and, ultimately, shape the culture of an organization. In some organizations, a smell of citrus, like Windex, permeates the air. Interestingly, this smell actually improves the behaviour of employees.

Specifically, as several research projects have uncovered, the scent of citrus actually promotes moral behaviour. In one study, for example, some participants were exposed to this scent, while other participants were not. If individuals had been exposed to citrus, they were subsequently more likely to donate money to a cause (Lilenquist, Zhong & Galinsky 2010).

Arguably, this aroma tends to correspond to hygiene. This citric smell, therefore, evokes memories of hygiene and purity. Individuals tend to associate this purity with innocence and morality. Therefore, even exposure to this scent is sufficient to promote moral behaviour, and employees are more inclined to behave ethically and collaboratively with one another.

✓ If an aroma of citrus, like Windex, pervades the air, employees are more likely to behave ethically and cooperatively.

Part C

Research Before the Interview

Chapter 6

Vision and values

Before you apply, you decide to visit the organization. As you enter the foyer, you observe a framed poster mounted proudly on the wall. The poster is entitled 'Our values'. Below the heading is a series of phrases: excellence and perfection; integrity and honesty; passion and commitment. These phrases are superimposed on a photograph of some young, trendy employees, seemingly creating an innovative product. These values seem appropriate, apart from one nagging doubt…

Often, in the foyer or in the offices, managers attach posters that specify the vision and values of the organization. The same information might appear on the website, on brochures, or in other official documents.

The vision statement encapsulates the ambitions and aspirations the organization would like to achieve. Typical statements include: 'To be the most efficient supplier of paper', or 'to be the provider of choice for dental services'. The values represent the qualities and characteristics that are perceived as moral and important – like integrity, reliability, safety, cooperation, innovation, excellence and efficiency.

Many variants have recently surfaced. Employee value propositions, for example, that specify the key benefits that employees will enjoy provided they fulfill the standards and expectations of the organization. Regardless of the precise format, references to values can be more consequential, and sometimes more harmful, than managers anticipate.

The perfect storm

Perhaps the most cherished item in the household is the TV remote control, closely followed by the dog, cat and children. This instrument is called a remote control because, once lost, the likelihood you will retrieve this item is remote.

The remote control also exemplifies a personality trait in many people. Specifically, some individuals do not press the buttons excessively. That is, once they uncover a program they like, they no longer feel the need to change the channel.

In contrast, other individuals press the buttons almost habitually. They switch from one channel to another channel, almost too rapidly to recognize the show. They are not satisfied with merely an acceptable alternative. They feel the need to uncover the best possible TV show on the planet.

These individuals tend to extend this inclination to other domains of their life. They scrutinize the menu at restaurants carefully, comparing and contrasting each item with one another until they uncover the best meal. In clothes stores, they appraise every item several times until they can optimize their decision.

Perhaps unsurprisingly, although they attempt to unearth the best option rather than merely accept a satisfactory alternative, these individuals are often not satisfied. Indeed, this attempt to optimize or perfect every choice has been shown to compromise satisfaction and to evoke negative emotions: anxiety, disappointment and regret, for example. The wellbeing of these individuals declines. Their satisfaction with life diminishes (Schwartz *et al.* 2002).

Unfortunately, some organizations merely reinforce this outlook. In their official documents, they allude to the importance of perfection. They denounce flaws. Slogans on the wall might read: 'We always get it right the first time'. The vision and values statement might refer to precision and perfection. The managers do not appreciate that errors are inevitable in organizations and integral to learning.

In one accounting firm located in Los Angeles, the manager considered every decision exhaustively and intensely. One day, for example, he decided the organization should purchase a sign that instructs visitors to 'push' the front door. He considered every possible combination of every possible feature. Should the plate consist of steel or tin? Should the letters be uppercase or lowercase? Should the background be green or red? Should the orientation be portrait or landscape? Should he include an icon of a hand or an arrow? Eventually, after several weeks, he finally reached a decision. Unfortunately, the sign was fastened to the wrong side of the door – the side from which visitors are supposed to pull.

When perfection is enforced, employees feel they need to optimize every decision. They feel afraid they might commit an error, a mindset that compromises their own mental health and diminishes their job satisfaction.

> ✖ One of the key values of some organizations revolves around perfection. In official documents or posters, flaws or mistakes are derided. In these organizations, you may not feel as inspired to experiment with various tasks. Your development might be stalled, and your contributions may be limited. Furthermore, managers that demand perfection on some days may demand productivity on other days – exposing a conflict in standards.

Obligation free

Many of the mottos, slogans or taglines that organizations embrace can exacerbate these problems. Some mottos are trite proverbs that appear on prints or posters such as: 'Where there's a will, there's a way', or 'an ounce of prevention is worth a pound of cure'. Other mottos might have been developed by the organization itself and appear on official documentation, such as annual reports, tender applications and marketing paraphernalia.

Obviously, the characteristics, climate and culture of an organization do not always align to the corporate slogan. For example, the motto of a workgroup in one New Zealand company, visible on posters that are scattered throughout the building, is 'Our creativity is unrivaled'. This motto, however, does not indicate the workgroup is actually creative – and, judging by the slogan, does not seem to be creative at all.

Although not especially accurate, these mottos or slogans of organizations, departments or teams are very revealing. Specifically, some mottos will affect the behaviour of individuals. That is, slogans can actually incite unintended behaviours and inclinations.

To illustrate, some mottos – such as 'an ounce of prevention is worth a pound of cure', 'better safe than sorry', or 'we never forget who we're working for' – emphasize caution and responsibility. That is, these mottos are intended to deter shortfalls, advocating care and vigilance instead.

When employees are exposed to these mottos, they indeed become more cautious (Faddegon, Scheepers & Ellemers 2008). Their primary motivation is to minimize errors rather than pursue opportunities. That is, they attempt to prevent deviations from some established routine or imposed standard. They orient their attention more to their immediate duties instead of to their future aspirations.

If employees embrace this motivation, they are indeed unlikely to commit as many errors, and are more inclined to satisfy their duties and responsibilities.

Nevertheless, this motivation also incites many complications. When individuals strive merely to fulfill their pressing duties, they neglect broader concerns (Forster & Higgins 2005). Consequently, they are likely to become more agitated, irritable or defensive. In response to unexpected changes or unforeseen obstacles, they become especially disconcerted and troubled (Kross & Ayduk 2008). If their colleagues undertake activities that deviate from the established practices, they often become irate or enraged. If their work is criticized, they frequently seem unreasonably defensive.

In contrast, some mottos – such as 'where there's a will, there's a way', 'dreams made real', 'pushing limits', or 'be everything you can be' – emphasize hope and opportunity. These mottos are intended to inspire employees to pursue risky but inspiring goals. When employees are exposed to these mottos, they are not as concerned about modest errors or problems. Indeed, they recognize that mistakes, shortfalls and complications are inevitable consequences of challenging endeavors. They realize that problems and obstacles symbolize progress and development.

In these environments, individuals do not only tolerate changes, criticism and complications, but they are also more likely to fulfill meaningful and inspiring goals. In particular, in this state, as they contemplate their opportunities in the future, they recognize the core purpose of diverse goals. Suddenly, all the activities they undertake – that is, all the roles in their life – seem to align to the same overarching aspiration or pursuit (Freitas *et al.* 2009). These activities and roles immediately feel important instead of peripheral. Their life seems meaningful instead of tenuous.

> ✓ Sometimes, the main slogan or motto of the company, department or team emphasizes the importance of pursuing inspiring aspirations in the remote future. Employees are encouraged to embrace the risks, complications and mistakes that growth and meaning often entails. If these slogans are prominent, the work and role is more likely to feel meaningful and important. You are also likely to feel a greater sense of control (Langens 2007).

Young at heart

In addition to particular slogans, the overarching brand can also orient attention to risks instead of caution. According to marketing experts, every brand – including makes of cars, food and toasters – exhibits a distinct personality. Initially, this concept might elicit an unusual image. Perhaps you can imagine a marketing guru with one arm around her toaster saying: 'I know he looks a bit ugly, but he's got a great personality'.

Nevertheless, organizations devote hundreds of thousands of dollars to the pursuit of a suitable personality. Some brands, for example, are perceived as daring and funky. Other brands may be perceived as simple, warm, moral, powerful, optimistic, thoughtful or serene.

Despite this diversity, the personality of brands can roughly be divided into two categories. First, some brands are regarded as more conservative and reliable. Customers tend to perceive these brands as wholesome, moral, traditional, prudent, dependable, cautious, thorough, sturdy, valid or precise. When customers purchase such brands – e.g. Volvo or Hallmarks – they do not anticipate any complications. They presume that these products or services will resolve, rather than exacerbate, their problems.

Second, some brands are regarded as more youthful and risky. Customers tend to perceive these brands as trendy, innovative, dynamic, exciting, thrilling and progressive. When customers purchase such brands – e.g. Virgin, Google or Apple – they anticipate inventive, diverse and helpful features. That is, customers are more inclined to seek originality and excitement than to demand perfection and precision.

Because the customers of these youthful, risky brands do not seek perfection, they seem to be more willing to tolerate complications or problems. One study, for example, examined the responses of customers to the errors of companies. That is, in general, when organizations commit an error, such as misplace an order, the customers are frustrated. Their loyalty declines, and they are not as inclined to purchase goods or services from this company in the future.

However, if the brand is youthful and risky, this problem subsides (Aaker, Fournier & Brasel 2004). Despite the errors, customers often remain loyal. They are not as concerned with temporary complications or problems.

Consequently, when the organization has cultivated a youthful and risky brand, managers do not always demand perfection from employees. If they commit an error, employees will not be castigated as harshly, and they will not be penalized or demoted.

Employees, therefore, do not feel as anxious or vigilant. They feel they can explore novel approaches, unconcerned with the trivial complications that inevitably unfold. They are more likely to develop their skills and expertise rather than remain stagnant and uninspired.

✓ The brands of some companies seem youthful, trendy and risky. Advertising material, for example, tends to depict younger people, perhaps engaged in active and risky ventures. In these companies, you are likely to feel you can develop your expertise without apprehension or anxieties about failures. You will feel you can contribute your distinct skills or unique attributes to the organization

Values without morals

Finally, some advertising material or vision and value statements emphasize prestige rather than perfection. For example, in a recent advertisement one company maintained that 'everyone is talking about our products'. Presumably, if this claim were true, they wouldn't need to advertise.

Indeed, many companies like to inflate their status, prestige or reputation. They may proclaim, for example, they are the market leader in their particular field.

Organizations that exaggerate their status, prestige and reputation tend to value achievement and power more than cooperation and responsibility. Interestingly, and despite these values, these organizations are not especially effective or influential. For example, when organizations emphasize achievement and power, particular circuits in the brain, and especially in the right hemisphere, are likely to be inhibited (Kuhl & Kazen 2008). When these circuits are inhibited, a spate of problems can unfold.

First, employees become uncooperative. Their motivation to help and to accommodate other people subsides. These uncooperative inclinations do not only undermine relationships and teamwork, but they can also impede progress and disrupt performance. When individuals are uncooperative, their capacity to negotiate effectively diminishes, and they cannot reach agreements that support the needs and interests of both parties (Butler 1999).

Second, when these circuits in the right hemisphere are inhibited, insight and creativity are also compromised. Innovation is stymied, and hence progress is curtailed. As a result, solutions become banal, and intractable problems linger (Beeman & Bowden 2000).

Problems such as ineffective negotiation or limited innovation are not as rife in organizations that value cooperation and responsibility over competition and power. The question, then, becomes one of how to ascertain these values. How can applicants determine whether the organization prioritizes competition over cooperation?

In many organizations, the publicized values – values like creativity, safety, honesty or responsibility – do not significantly govern the practices, procedures or products of organizations. That is, organizations that supposedly value innovation do not invariably institute practices that actually fulfill this priority. Organizations that apparently value morality and safety are often riskier than competitors (McKendall, DeMarr & Jones-Rikkers 2002).

Indeed, many employees cannot even recite the values of their organization. In one IT company located in New York, a sample of 100 employees were asked to specify the values of their organization. Although these values were broadcast conspicuously in the foyer, 95 of these employees conceded they did not know the answer. Only four of these employees responded with the phrase 'Save money, live better' – actually the slogan of Walmart at the time – but a reasonable effort nonetheless.

Regardless, these values do offer some insight into the culture and climate of organizations. In general, although not invariably, the value that is listed first or second is often more likely to epitomize the organization than is the value that is listed last or second last. That is, when managers generate these values, the most accessible priorities – the priorities they actually embrace – tend to be identified first (Fitzsimons & Shah 2008). If the organization actually values achievement over integrity, priorities like excellence or performance will often be evoked first. Priorities like sincerity or honesty are likely to be evoked later. In other words, the order in which individuals entertain thoughts, and thus express their opinions, can be very telling.

Furthermore, the values are sometimes listed in a column. In these instances, values at the top are perceived by employees as more important than values at the bottom. That is, individuals tend to attach more importance, significance or trust to words that are high, rather than low, in space (Meier, Sellbom & Wygant 2007). They are more likely to comply with the values that appear at the top of this inventory.

> ✻ Many organizations will specify their values on posters and other formats, often in a column. If values that relate to competition, achievement, excellence and performance precede values that relate to respect, honesty, conservation and safety, then the organization may be too competitive and unsupportive.

Chapter 7

Senior managers and directors

As you visit the website, you click on a link called 'Executives'. A list of names and titles appear, like John Smith, CEO; Sally Jones, Managing Director; Ian Brown, Director; Betty Anderson, Director. As you click on the various names, you read their biographies, most of which seem impressive but uninformative. The CEO, for example, was assigned this position three years ago, after working at the organization since 1990. The directors are also members of many other boards in a variety of industries. On the website is also a photograph of the senior managers and directors, all wearing their elegant, dark suits. At first glance, the information does not seem especially telling. After a while, you become aware of two important problems...

On websites, in annual reports or from other documents, you can often garner some information about the senior managers, with titles like CEO, CFO, regional manager, and the like. In large companies you may also be able to distil information about the directors, including perhaps the chair, president or managing director. Obviously, to the untrained observer, these biographies will seem uninteresting. Salacious details about previous infidelities, corporate fraud or unusual diseases are unlikely to be included. Nevertheless, some of these details often correlate with grave concerns.

The senior novice

Whenever a CEO is replaced by another person, shareholders often feel buoyant and excited. Perhaps, after some delay, they anticipate a surge in growth and profit, followed by an escalation in the value of their shares.

In recent years, however, scientists have demonstrated that such optimism is often unfounded. In general, when one CEO departs and another person is appointed, performance of the organization will tend to improve transiently and then wane afterwards (Hughes *et al.* 2010). Profit may increase in the first three months, but then plateau and even decline over the next year. Sales might proliferate for one month or so, but then they diminish.

As performance declines, this CEO may be quickly replaced. Again, performance of the organization will improve briefly and then deteriorate gradually. This pattern may even last indefinitely.

Several explanations have been proposed to explain this initial spike in workplace performance. First, when a fresh CEO begins, a variety of changes may unfold: the existing employees might feel the need to demonstrate their value; or they might, at least initially, work more productively or innovatively.

Second, some ventures may have been delayed until this CEO was appointed. That is, managers might have decided to defer some of their programs, primarily to ensure the successor will also endorse the initiatives. Once this CEO begins, these initiatives are more likely to be implemented, and workplace performance might initially improve.

Third, even the prospect of change can elicit positive emotions and attitudes. In the midst of change, individuals often feel more excited and not dejected. They are more inclined to experiment with suggestions rather than prevaricate needlessly. They are even more willing to embrace other changes and initiatives (e.g. Wood 2010).

Nevertheless, after this initial lift, problems begin to mount. Specifically, despite the feelings of hope, few CEOs usually appreciate the underlying and overarching causes of problems. They are seldom aware of the primary origins of most workplace complications: inconsistent standards or expectations, a competitive mindset, unpredictable adversities, and limited opportunities to develop specialized skills. They do not, therefore, redress the source of decline. Thus, once the original excitement fades, these complications accrue and performance wanes.

In addition, within their first year many CEOs attempt to introduce a vision of the work environment – a wholesale change to the existing strategies. They might, for example, institute a novel means to appraise performance, or they might promulgate a supposedly unique series of values, like innovation, responsibility and performance.

These attempts, however, are often futile. First, when a fresh CEO begins, employees often feel uncertain and even uneasy. They are not certain what changes to expect. They are not sure whether they will embrace the new regime. When employees feel uneasy and uncertain, their attention is directed primarily to more immediate concerns, and they are not as likely to consider their future goals and objectives.

Consequently, a vision of the future does not resonate with their needs. They do not feel inspired, and might even feel alienated. Indeed, as research shows, employees are often offended by these strategies (Sparrowe, Soetjipto & Kraimer 2006). They feel as if their previous endeavours and established practices have been scorned. They will, therefore, often reject the changes, compromising performance.

Thus, a few months after an existing CEO has been replaced, performance will often deteriorate. Expenses might need to be curtailed. Many plans are abandoned or even discarded altogether. The environment seems unpredictable and uninspiring.

✓ If the CEO has been assigned this position for over two years, work practices, policies and procedures are not as likely to change erratically and incessantly. You are more likely to feel a sense of control.

Succession and success

Companies often like to emphasize the quality of their managers and employees. They like to maintain that they attract the most skilled, talented, insightful, creative and responsible individuals, certainly more proficient than employees and managers at rival organizations. Yet despite this contention, companies often recruit CEOs from outside the organization. If these companies attract the most talented people, they should be able to promote someone from within the organization.

Actually, when CEOs are recruited from outside the organization, performance is more likely to decline, at least two or three years later, as studies demonstrate (Zhang & Rajagopalan 2004). That is, compared to CEOs who were groomed to lead within the organization, CEOs enticed from other companies tend to initiate more changes. They are not as likely to understand the benefits of practices that, at first glance, might seem inefficient or obsolete. They are not as likely to appreciate the programs and initiatives the organization had recently introduced. That is, the existing practices and programs seem unfamiliar to CEOs recruited from outside the organization. Unfamiliar practices and programs tend to be perceived unfavorably, even if actually effective.

In one rail company, located in London, within three months of his appointment, the CEO decided to abandon many existing programs and introduce an initiative called 'work reduction', intended to decrease unnecessary work demands. Within one week, almost five percent of the employees decided to leave the organization. The share price plummeted. Unfortunately, the CEO was not aware that 20 percent of employees had been retrenched the previous year, and this retrenchment process had been called 'work reduction' as well.

Because these CEOs initiate many changes, employees experience a sense of uncertainty. They cannot be certain whether other practices or procedures will be abandoned in the future. As this uncertainty prevails, they feel more vulnerable. They overreact to trivial complications and impediments. As investigations have shown, CEOs recruited from outside the organization are particularly likely to undermine performance when the industry is unstable or competitive (Zhang & Rajagopalan 2004).

In contrast, when CEOs are recruited from existing managers, these problems are not as likely. The CEO does not institute a vast series of disruptive changes, and the work environment feels more predictable and stable.

> ✓ Sometimes, you can calculate that the CEO worked at the organization before assuming this position. For example, the CEO might have occupied this role since 2006, but worked at their previous organization until 2002. In these instances, policies and practices are unlikely to change too dramatically, enabling employees to experience a sense of control.

The concrete ceiling

The scarcity of women on boards is like a pile of manure on the sidewalk: everyone knows it stinks but nobody really wants to intervene. In many nations, the percentage of males on boards exceeds 90 percent.

Indeed, the men on most boards tend to be quite masculine: bold, assertive, forceful and unfeeling. Emotional, effeminate, and even thin men are not as likely to occupy boards of management. As research shows, thin men, compared to other males, are not as likely to be granted positions of power and privilege: their income tends to be modest (Judge & Cable 2011).

Organizations that are teeming with male, rather than female, executives – especially strong, conceited or aggressive men – are often plagued with a particular array of consequential problems. First, in contrast to women, strong and brash men often embrace unnecessary risks. They are more inclined to seek risks. They enjoy the thrill that uncertainty and opportunity can provoke. Indeed, as research shows, if the hand grip of a person is particularly strong, they are more likely to seek thrilling and even dangerous activities (Fink *et al.* 2010).

Therefore, when most of the executives are strong, conceited and aggressive men, workplace performance often varies erratically and sometimes dramatically. Sometimes, because these managers embrace risks, their decisions appreciably enhance the value and the profit of the firm. On other occasions, however, these decisions can be disastrous. Remedial interventions, often in the form of downsizing, are warranted. Employees are retrenched, workgroups are restructured, and uncertainty prevails. The workplace seems unpredictable, and the wellbeing of employees is threatened.

Second, when the boards are replete with strong, conceited and aggressive men, the work environment is competitive but often unproductive. That is, as research indicates, the personality of executives affects the culture of workplaces.

Specifically, when the executives are assertive, aggressive or uncompromising, the managers that report to these individuals are not as inclined to cooperate with each other (Peterson *et al.* 2003). These managers feel the need to accommodate the needs of these dominant executives. Their attention, therefore, is oriented towards the preferences of executives instead of the needs of peers or subordinates. These managers, therefore, also behave assertively, and sometimes aggressively, to subordinates. This assertive, competitive and aggressive mindset then perpetuates down the hierarchy, and the work environment, in general, is uncooperative and unsupportive.

Obviously, not all males are aggressive and competitive – or even assertive and strong. Similarly, not all females are cooperative, sensitive or kind. Nevertheless, in general men are often more competitive, and less cooperative, than women. When most, if not all, of the executives are male, the work environment is more likely to be unpredictable and uncooperative. When many of the executives are female, the conditions are usually more favorable.

> ✓ In some organizations, a significant portion of the board members or senior managers are female – perhaps 40 percent or more. These organizations tend to be steadier and more supportive. You are more likely to feel a feeling of control as well as a sense of cohesion within the workgroup or department.

Dropping the ball

During a job interview, over the telephone, an applicant asks the managing director: 'Did you have your wisdom teeth out yesterday?' The director answers: 'No, why would you think that?' The applicant replied: 'It's just that your personal assistant mentioned you have a swollen head, so I just assumed you had'.

The senior personnel of companies – the directors, CEOs, general managers, and the like – often attempt to inflate their experience and reputation. In official documents, like annual reports or websites, they often like to demonstrate their vast experience. They might, for example, specify their extensive array of previous roles in other companies. They may allude to the years, or even decades, of service they have dedicated to this industry. They may also catalog all the other boards or associations of which they are now a member.

Although sometimes compelling, this experience does not always translate into wisdom. Two complications permeate many organizations today.

First, if these managers are not especially happy or content, their decisions are often misguided, despite their experience.

Specifically, after many years of service in a role or industry, managers learn which practices and behaviours are effective and useful in various settings. When their colleagues tend to be reserved, an assertive approach might be more useful. When their colleagues tend to competitive, a more obliging style might be preferable. They discover that many subtle features, such as the mood of colleagues or the time of year, affect the consequences of their behaviour – too many features to be analyzed consciously. Instead, they recognize these patterns and regularities unconsciously.

In essence, the intuition of individuals represents these unconscious insights. Therefore, to reach suitable decisions, especially in unpredictable settings, individuals need to utilize their intuition. They need to trust their hunches. They cannot merely apply a series of principles, like 'managers should be firm but fair' or 'managers should diversify their investments', to improve their business. These sweeping principles are not suitable to all contexts, and these assumptions are insensitive to the complexities and constraints of the environment.

Nevertheless, unless individuals feel happy, content or other pleasant but soothing emotions, they cannot utilize their intuition effectively (e.g. Hicks et al. 2010). Negative feelings, such as dejection or agitation, tend to inhibit the brain circuits that facilitate intuition. Specifically, when individuals feel dejected, they tend to apply inflexible principles instead of their intuitive hunches. When individuals feel agitated, their intuition is supplanted by more primal instincts. Their decisions often neglect future implications and optimize only their immediate needs.

Studies have, indeed, shown that experience does not translate into wisdom unless individuals can utilize their intuition. Perhaps the most interesting study examined decisions in the domain of sport (Dijksterhuis et al. 2009). In this study, individuals were asked to predict which football team would prevail in a particular contest. Some of the individuals had acquired extensive knowledge about the sport, watching hundreds of games over many years. Other individuals were not as experienced. They had not watched many games at all.

In addition, some of the participants were instructed to apply systematic principles. For example, they could collate and count the benefits and drawbacks of each team. Other participants were invited to utilize their intuition. That is, they were encouraged to consider the teams briefly, distract themselves with another engaging activity, and then trust any intuitions or hunches that unfold over time.

If participants applied systematic principles, the level of experience was unrelated to the accuracy of their predictions. People who had watched football extensively were no more likely than people who had watched football only sporadically, if at all, to forecast the victor correctly. However, if participants utilized their intuition, in a composed state, experience was beneficial. The people who had watched football extensively were especially likely to predict the victor accurately.

If intuition is invoked, experience is beneficial. Experienced managers will reach suitable decisions. The organization, therefore, will advance steadily rather than vary erratically.

✓ In some organizations, the senior managers seem content and satisfied. In photographs, for example, their smiles seem genuine rather than contrived. Furthermore, their profiles may refer to interests or hobbies that promote serenity and contentment, like fishing or bushwalking. In these organizations, you are unlikely to feel vulnerable to unexpected demands and complications. Instead, you may experience a sense of control and security.

A second complication is that managers who participate on many boards, either as directors or advisors, are often not committed enough to any specific endeavor. That is, if managers dedicate most of their time to one or two companies or boards, they feel more committed to these pursuits. In contrast, if managers distribute their time across many companies or boards, they often do not feel as committed to any one of these pursuits.

Although this diversity might extend their knowledge, these managers do tend to withhold some effort. These individuals seldom, for example, read the relevant material before the board meetings are convened. They do not, usually, strive to garner other sources of information as well. During meetings, perhaps because their information is limited, these managers are not as likely to intervene constructively or pose important questions.

Systematic investigations have confirmed this account (Minichilli, Zattoni & Zona 2009). For example, in one study, 301 CEOs of large Italian companies completed a questionnaire. First, these CEOs completed a variety of questions that assessed whether the board of directors was functioning effectively. They were, for example asked to indicate the extent to which the board offers useful advice on finances, taxation, technology, consumers, strategy, and other matters. In addition, they were asked to specify whether the board enhances the reputation or esteem of the organization as well facilitates relationships with other stakeholders. Furthermore, they indicated the degree to which the board monitors and evaluates strategic initiatives and core activities.

Second, these CEOs were also asked to indicate the degree to which members of the board are committed to their role. That is, they were asked to gauge whether or not these board members scrutinize information before meetings, seek other sources of insight, dedicate time to other board activities, and raise constructive questions during meetings. The results were unambiguous: if the members were not committed to this endeavor, the boards were not especially useful.

This problem is epitomized by an American manufacturer of computer hardware such as external hard drives. The directors of this company were inattentive, distracted by their own interests elsewhere. In two years, profit diminished from $100 million to a loss, primarily because the CEO and CFO had siphoned the money to personal accounts.

When one of the directors was asked by journalists why the decline in profit had not evoked suspicion, he replied: 'We just felt that external hard drives may not be as popular anymore'. Either this director was not aware that sales in external hard drives had actually soared during this period – or the director had confused external hard drives with the 3 ¾ inch disks they had used a decade ago.

> ✘ In some companies, the directors are members of two or more other boards. When directors are members of too many boards, the organization is not managed effectively, unexpected problems often unfold, and the work environment often seems unsteady and unpredictable.

Chapter 8

Executive announcements and communication

On the website of this organization, you download a
newsletter. In this newsletter, the CEO began with the
sentence: 'I trust you enjoyed your break, but are still
excited about the year ahead'. She then specified all the
money the company had donated to a cause: a fund that
was developed to assist ill children. Nevertheless, she
conceded that profit had diminished. She suggested that
had she decided to invest more heavily in training, profit
could have increased instead. Finally, she pledged to
increase investment, rather than reduce expenses, over
the next year. You acknowledge the benefits of her
report, but then unearth one unfavourable feature...

At the premises or on the website of organizations, the public
can often access some of the messages and announcements of
executives and managers. In a newsletter, for example, the
managing director might describe some recent or imminent
ventures. In the annual report, the CEO might reflect upon
some of the complications they plan to redress in the future.
Their accounts are often biased, and their pledges are usually
inflated. Nevertheless, a careful examination can uncover some
important insights – insights the managers had not intended.

Hidden love

In general, hippies are not the most successful executives. The
managing director or CEO of a thriving company is unlikely to

articulate, in an annual report, newsletter or bulletin that people should 'Drop acid, not bombs' and 'Make love, not war'.

However, as scientists have demonstrated, subtle references to words that symbolize support, like 'love', can be very beneficial. That is, some managers, in official reports or even everyday conversations, will utilize words that epitomize support, including 'care', 'nurture', 'help', 'assist', 'trust' and 'love'. They might express comments like 'I really care about this project', 'we need to nurture these qualities', 'I can't help feel excited about this possibility', 'I might be able to assist you', 'I trust that everything is fine', and 'I love your attitude'. Although none of these remarks are especially tender, they each include a word that symbolizes support.

When individuals are exposed to these words, they are, for some reason, more inclined to concede their limitations or admit to errors. When problems transpire, they assume responsibility, if applicable. Because of this candor, these individuals are not defensive. Instead, they tend to be poised and resilient. The environment is more likely to be collaborative and predictable.

Some exciting research does attest to the benefits of these words. In one example, participants were exposed to subliminal words – that is, words that were presented too rapidly to be recognized consciously. Some of these participants were exposed to words that epitomize support, like 'love'. Other participants were exposed to unemotional words, like 'table'.

Next, participants were instructed to list some of their strengths, limitations, or occasions in which they felt they had acted inappropriately or shamefully. If these individuals had been exposed to words that epitomize support, they were more inclined to concede limitations or shameful behaviours (Gillath *et al.* 2010).

These words diminished their apprehension about relationships. They felt trusting instead of insecure. Consequently, they did not experience the need to conceal their problems. They felt they could be honest and sincere.

> ✖ In annual reports, newsletters, speeches and other settings, some managers, even if inadvertently, utilize words that epitomize support, like 'care', 'nurture', 'help', 'assist', 'trust' and 'love'. Employees who hear these words are more likely to disclose their anxieties, reducing the likelihood of defensive, volatile or hostile behaviour at the workplace. At these organizations, you are more likely to experience a sense of control.

Unhelpful help

Besides this inadvertent support, managers sometimes deliberately allude to charitable behaviour. In most annual reports, newsletters, bulletins or other forums, the CEO or some other executive will attempt to depict the organization as a responsible, cooperative and humane environment. Even if, in practice, these managers actually mug small children throughout the day, they will still allude to their philanthropic or altruistic activities.

Most organizations now contribute to many social causes such as homeless youth or environmental protection. Nevertheless, at least sometimes the motivation of managers is primarily to enhance the reputation of their organization. They are not always genuinely passionate about this cause.

In the UK, for example, one cigarette company wanted to donate money to support research into cancer. They were not so concerned about the welfare of their customers, however they did not donate money to support campaigns that curb the addiction to cigarettes.

Research has recently verified this cynicism (Griskevicius, Tybur & Van den Bergh 2010). For example, in one study participants read a short story, comprising approximately 700 words, about a college student who wanted to ascend the corporate hierarchy. This story was intended to emphasize the importance of status. That is, after reading this anecdote, participants are more inclined to covet status and prestige. Other participants, in contrast, read a story that was similar in length but did not refer to status.

Next, participants received information about two cars, household cleaners and dishwashers. For each pair of items, one of the alternatives was prestigious but not designed to conserve the environment; the other product was not as prestigious, but was intended to conserve the environment. The dishwasher that was designed to conserve the environment, for example, was manufactured from recycled materials and also reused the water.

After participants read a story about status and prestige, they were more inclined to purchase the alternatives that were designed to conserve the environment. As this study indicates, individuals sometimes enact responsible or altruistic behaviours to enhance their status. That is, throughout every civilization, only affluent organizations or individuals can afford to direct their wealth to philanthropic or altruistic projects. If the organization is not thriving, such endeavors are usually curtailed. Therefore, to feign success and to attract investors, managers often dedicate significant sums of money to charitable activities.

At first glance, this state of affairs might seem to be symbiotic. Managers are able to inflate their status; the recipients of this support are able to improve their lives. Everyone prospers.

Unfortunately, in practice, philanthropic activities or community work that is, primarily, motivated by the need to enhance the status and prestige of the organization is often ineffective – and sometimes even destructive. Specifically, as research illustrates, in these circumstances, two complications undermine the assistance these organizations offer (Nadler, Harpaz-Gorodeisky & Ben-David 2009). First, when organizations strive to enhance their status, they seldom fulfill the needs, or resolve the problems, of the communities they attempt to assist. That is, they are often insensitive to the specific needs of these communities. Even if unintentional, they undertake activities that are simple and conspicuous rather than helpful and essential.

For example, in one community, ongoing disputes and divisions precluded collaboration and impede progress. Rather than facilitate the resolution of these disputes, one large Australian company merely donated huge sums of money. These sums of money, however, merely exacerbated the divisions and damaged the community. The various constituencies of the community could not agree on who should administer these funds.

Second, and perhaps more interestingly, when organization strive to enhance their status, they often, either deliberately or inadvertently, increase the dependence of this community on the assistance they offer. They might, for example, mediate disputes. They will not, however, impart the knowledge that is needed to enable these communities to resolve these conflicts themselves. They might donate funds, but not enhance the capacity of these communities to earn and to manage this money in the future. Over time, the recipients of their assistance become more reliant instead of autonomous.

In short, some organizations appear to be philanthropic and responsible. Nevertheless, these activities, in one sense, are partly a ruse, intended to enhance the status and prestige of these companies. These activities are not only futile, at least in some instances, but also do not indicate the organization is cooperative and communal. That is, despite this community support, the culture of this company might be competitive, unsupportive and even ruthless.

To establish whether these charitable activities are genuine, four principles should be considered. First, when these activities are described, managers should describe, in vivid detail, the needs and concerns of the recipient. If the organization supports homeless youth, managers should refer to some of the key challenges these individuals need to resolve: perhaps family conflict, shame, and frostbite, for example. If the organization wants to assist recent migrants, the managers should also allude to the problems and issues these individuals need to address. These managers need to show they are sensitive to the needs of these communities.

> ✓ Sometimes, in an annual report, newsletter, or some other forum, the managers describe the challenges and complications that particular communities need to resolve as well as initiatives the organization introduced to fulfill this goal. That is, the manager exhibits sensitivity and understanding while describing some charitable activity. This sensitivity in managers indicates the support is probably genuine rather than merely an attempt to reinforce their status. The managers, therefore, are likely to be supportive and considerate.

Second, this report or account should, if applicable, allude to some injustice – an injustice the organization would like to redress. Perhaps the report could refer to the rampant prejudice that is sweeping the nation. Alternatively, the report, or some other memorandum, might allude to the inadequate aged care or the deficient support of political refugees prevalent in many regions. That is, the organization should be dedicated to some campaign or injustice. Activism should be embraced rather than shunned.

Research has confirmed the benefits of this commitment to activism – the benefits of these gallant attempts to redress injustices. Specifically, when employees read these reports, they are more inclined to feel alert, energetic, spirited and vitalized (Klar & Kasser 2010), and are not as likely to feel exhausted or overwhelmed.

Consequently, in these workplaces, employees are not as likely to be abrupt or aggressive. They can inhibit any unsuitable inclinations or hostile thoughts, and cohesion and cooperation tend to flourish and thrive.

> ✓ Occasionally, in an annual report, newsletter, or some other forum, the managers describes some

> injustice in the world – an injustice that disadvantages a deprived or impaired community. These accounts tend to enhance engagement and reduce the likelihood of outbursts or uncooperative behaviour at work. The environment seem cooperative and supportive.

Third, managers should refer to initiatives that were intended to enhance the independence, and thus curb the vulnerability, of some community. Perhaps the organization had convened a series of workshops, programs or courses that enhance the skills of people in this community. That is, the organization might have imparted constructive, substantiated insights – insights the community could not have acquired otherwise.

Nevertheless, despite these attempts to instill this independence, the managers should also maintain their commitment to this community, evaluating progress and offering feedback to sustain these changes. They should not, obviously, abandon the cause once these programs have been implemented. They should ensure their programs are maintained and refined over time.

> ✓ In annual reports, newsletters, and other formats, the managers sometimes refer to activities that curb the reliance of these communities on outside assistance, such as workshops. In addition, these managers also allude to initiatives that were implemented to ensure these programs were useful and sustained, such as regular evaluations and ongoing advice. These comments imply the charitable work was genuine. The managers, therefore, are likely to be kind and cooperative.

If only

In annual reports and other forms of communication, managers do not fixate exclusively on uplifting events, such as charitable events or sales growth. They may sometimes allude to unexpected challenges or grave disappointments.

Managers will often consider how events could have unfolded differently, called counterfactuals. Sometimes, they may write about how the performance or progress of the organization could have been less favorable. They might write, for example: 'Although our revenue diminished, if we had not invested wisely last year, we might not have been profitable at all'.

On other occasions, managers write about how the performance or progress of the organization could have been better. They could contend that: 'Although we generated a profit, if we had not diversified our operations, our revenue might have increased'.

In this example, the manager alluded to an activity the organization did undertake but should have withheld. That is, the manager implied the operations should not have been diversified. In other instances, managers allude to additional activities the organization should have pursued. The manager might assert that: 'Although we generated a profit, if we had invested more in training, our revenue might have increased'.

These distinctions seem trivial and inconsequential. Whether or not managers allude to how performance could have been more favorable or less favorable – as well as whether specific activities should have been implemented or withdrawn – does not seem important. Yet, actually, these distinctions, although subtle, are significant.

In particular, effective managers will tend to refer to additional activities the organization should have pursued to improve the outlook. These managers seldom, if ever, emphasize how performance or progress could have been less favorable. In addition, these managers do not allude to activities that were undertaken but should have been withheld.

When managers consider additional activities the organization should have pursued to improve the outlook, several benefits unfold. First, these reflections have been shown to enhance creativity (Markman *et al.* 2007). When individuals consider additional activities they should have undertaken, instead of activities they should have withdrawn, circuits or mechanisms in the brain that facilitate creativity are activated. The managers, therefore, can uncover more creative, novel and effective solutions to solve important and intractable problems in the workplace. Challenges are resolved, and the environment is improved.

Second, if managers consider how performance could have been more favorable rather than less favorable, their mood deteriorates momentarily – a decline that increases their resolve and capacity to change. These managers, therefore, are willing to withstand the unpleasant emotions that deliberation might evoke. These individuals are considered and measured. They do not merely reach decisions that enhance their immediate emotions. They are thus not as likely to be impulsive and capricious.

Instead, these managers pursue courses of action that benefit the organization in the future. The organization is more likely to advance gradually rather than fluctuate unpredictably.

> ✓ In the annual report or similar documents, some managers are more inclined to allude to how performance could have been better than how performance could have been more unfavorable. Furthermore, they refer to activities that should have been attempted rather than activities that were initiated but should have been withheld. These managers tend to foster the capacity to resolve problems creatively, reducing the likelihood of problems and embracing innovation. You are likely to experience a sense of control and feel your contributions will be valued.

The unexpected costs of reducing expenses

Besides reflecting upon the past, managers often contemplate future goals in annual reports or other memoranda. Often, managers will emphasize the need to curb expenses. Each department, for example, might be assigned the role of reducing costs by, for example, 20 percent over the year.

To some extent, these organizations tend to resemble a person who has pledged to abstain from chocolate. They continue to behave as before – but just feel significantly guiltier each time.

When individuals and organizations strive deliberately to curtail expenses, several problems unfold. First, their budget forecasts tend to be inaccurate.

Specifically, individuals and organizations tend to overestimate the likelihood they will fulfill important but demanding goals. If they plan to complete a report in three weeks, they will usually need four weeks instead. If they plan to lose five kg in a month, they will probably lose fewer than 2.5 . If they plan to decrease expenses by 20 percent, they will most likely save less than five percent if anything .

In particular, when individuals pursue important but demanding goals, they need to feel very motivated and confident. Without this motivation or confidence, they will not persist doggedly. As soon as obstacles inhibit their progress, they will abandon their efforts.

To boost their motivation and confidence, people naturally orient their attention to their entrenched skills, desirable qualities and favorable opportunities. If they need to complete a report in three weeks, they might remember a time in which they fulfilled a similar goal in the past. If they plan to lose five kg in a month, they might fixate their concentration on the glowing recommendations of the weight loss program they have joined. If they decide to decrease expenses by 20 percent, they might direct their attention to some of their needless costs.

Their attention, therefore, is naturally biased towards promising opportunities rather than regrettable constraints. They neglect the possibility of unforeseen challenges: debilitating illness, wavering motivation, natural disasters, consequential mistakes, equipment malfunction, and many other concerns. In practice, therefore, their goals are not as viable as assumed. Their objectives are seldom realized on time, and their deadlines are not often fulfilled.

Controlled experiments have confirmed this complication. In one study, some participants were encouraged to save money. That is, they were informed that successful people tend to save money effectively. Other participants were not encouraged to save money: they were informed that successful people tend to spend liberally.

Next, every morning, over a week, participants were asked to record the money they plan to spend that day. Every evening, they recorded the money they *actually* spent that day.

If participants had been encouraged to save money, they were more likely to underestimate the amount of money they would spend (Peetz & Buehler 2009). These participants incorrectly predicted they would be thrifty. They had, presumably, oriented their attention to opportunities that could reduce their costs: perhaps their determination, for example. They may have, nevertheless, overlooked events that could escalate their costs, such as powerful urges to purchase clothes.

Therefore, when individuals and organizations strive resolutely to decrease expenses, budget forecasts, in general, are unduly optimistic. Expenses tend to exceed the targets. Goals are not fulfilled. The managers of these organizations, therefore, are usually frustrated, or even furious – sometimes withdrawing important endeavors in response. They might, for example, abandon some training initiative, shut an entire business unit, or initiate retrenchments. The organization becomes unsettled and unpredictable. Anxiety and uncertainty prevail, while progress and growth dissipate.

As an illustration, in one American company the CEO pledged to decrease the expenses of his organization by ten percent. He engaged a consultant to facilitate this goal. However, after one year, this target had not been achieved. Indeed, expenses actually increased by $35,000 – almost exactly the fee that was charged by the consultant. Consequently, the next year, the CEO merely retrenched ten percent of employees.

In addition to these concerns, whenever managers attempt to curb expenses, they tend to shun risk. They merely seek expenses or costs they can shrink rather than opportunities they can pursue. Innovation is eschewed, and creativity is not cherished (Forster & Higgins 2005). Employees do not feel as inspired to explore novel solutions, impeding their progress and development.

> ✔ In annual reports, or in other official documentation, managers sometimes emphasize their intention to decrease expenses appreciably over the next year. In these organizations, unpredictable complications are prevalent, and a sense of control therefore diminishes. Furthermore, your novel suggestions and distinct contributions are unlikely to be embraced.

Chapter 9

Budget and finances

The annual report, accessible from the website of this company, is replete with financial measures and indices. For example, a graph appears on one page, revealing the share price has gradually increased over the year. On another page is the remuneration of each director and senior manager, including their bonuses. Finally, other pages include various reports, from the managing director and CEO, for example. One report delineates the key activities of the organization last year, such as the merger with another company. Another report mentions the main objective next year: a decrease of ten percent in expenses. You feel this information is pleasing, apart from one disconcerting matter...

Public companies are obliged to publicize information about their finances. This information might appear in an annual report, prospectus for shareholders, or other documents, usually available on their website. Interestingly, some measures or indices, although encouraging to accountants, can actually indicate subtle problems in the organization.

A crying stock

When people leave their premises, they often hire a contractor or company to remove their furniture. These companies, unfortunately, often damage the walls or furnishings.

Last year, one couple hired a company that removed all their furniture without leaving a single trace. The couple would have been delighted, except they had actually employed this company to unblock the toilet. That is, one morning, after the contractors arrived, the couple left the house to attend work and returned that night, to discover to entire premises had been cleaned out – except, ironically enough, the toilet.

Although an appalling example, the practices of many companies are unethical, duplicitous and unlawful. These companies often strive to exploit, rather than to help, their clients.

Financial malfeasance, in which companies manipulate their financial statements, represents one of the most prevalent, as well as destructive, examples of unethical and unlawful practices. To illustrate, in some companies not all sales are recorded, primarily to decrease income tax. Alternatively, managers may accept surreptitious enticements from suppliers to purchase their products. Personal expenses are recoded as business outlays to diminish personal income tax. Money from illegal activities, like drugs, are recorded as legitimate entries, such as donations. Indeed, many other forms of fraud, misappropriation and embezzlement are rife.

In short, these practices distort their financial statements to favor specific personnel, such as the executives. These distortions are intended to mislead tax agencies, investors and other stakeholders.

At first glance, some employees are not too concerned about the prospect of working at a fraudulent organization. Unfortunately, these unjust or unlawful practices elicit several problems that ultimately compromise the wellbeing of employees.

For example, these fraudulent activities often correspond to a culture of secrecy and suspicion. To justify their behaviour, the managers that participate in these schemes form the assumption that dishonesty is rife. They like to feel their duplicity is prevalent and therefore acceptable. Their trust in other people thus abates. They might decide to monitor employees closely, and they might often accuse people of illicit behaviour.

A climate of mistrust and cynicism evolves. Employees do not feel the environment is cooperative. When complications in their life unfold, they do not feel they necessarily will be supported. Their anxieties often linger, and their mood deteriorates.

In addition, the environment often seems unpredictable. To illustrate, companies that engage in financial malfeasance often need to issue financial restatements. That is, after an audit or investigation, these companies frequently need to update the information they had distributed to various bodies, such as tax agencies. Employees often discover that some business activities are not as viable as they had assumed. Their department, for example, might not be as profitable as they had been informed, compromising their job security and eliciting anxiety.

Obviously, in job interviews managers are unlikely to confess to these practices. They are seldom inclined to remark: 'What's one of your main weaknesses – because mine is embezzlement'. Fortunately, researchers have shown that such financial malfeasance is more prevalent in specific contexts (Prechel & Morris 2010).

First, if the share or stock price of a company diminished significantly over the year, such unethical or unlawful practices are also more likely to unfold. Specifically, in these contexts, managers feel compelled to inflate the performance of their organization to attract institutional investors. Without these investors, credit can become more expensive. Intended initiatives cannot be implemented. Ultimately, the value of these companies might decline, often curtailing the bonuses, stock options or even reputations of managers.

> ✖ Financial statements, often accessible on the web, sometimes indicate the share price of an organization has, overall, decreased over the last year. Consequently, executives are more tempted to initiate financial malfeasance in which they distort these financial statements. In these companies, a

sense of distrust often pervades the environment. Furthermore, you might sometimes be informed that specific departments or activities are not as viable as you had assumed, diminishing your job security.

Mergers and mistrust

Second, companies often merge with each other. The two companies might agree to unite, primarily to form a more efficient or influential organization. Alternatively, one company might decide to purchase another company.

To illustrate, in the late 1990s, a company called Shay and another company called Dee People, both manufacturers of furniture, decided to form one organization. Unfortunately, these companies decided to combine their two names, oblivious to the problems that could unfold once they call themselves 'Shay Dee People'.

If the company has recently initiated a mergers or acquisition, illicit practices are more likely. In the midst of mergers and acquisitions, cash flow is constrained. That is, resources are diverted to logistical and administrative procedures. Inadequate cash or resources are available to fund other projects, impeding the performance of this organization.

To compensate, managers are often motivated to inflate the financial performance of their organization. That is, to maintain the reputation of this emerging company, despite their existing challenges, these managers attempt to overestimate the various indices of performance, such as profit. Financial malfeasance is thus more likely.

✖ In the annual report or some other document, companies may indicate they have recently undergone a merger or acquisition, perhaps in the last year or so. Often, after a merger and acquisition, financial malfeasance becomes more likely. Mistrust

> and job insecurity might have increased.

Finally, if the organization is a subsidiary of a massive corporation, financial malfeasance is also more common. Many companies are actually subsidiaries of other firms. That is, more than half the value of one company might be owned by another firm, but otherwise operates as an independent entity. These firms, in turn, might be subsidiaries of another parent company. This arrangement is called a multilayer subsidiary form.

Although not ubiquitous, financial malfeasance is more common in organizations that conform to this arrangement. In these arrangements, capital can readily be transferred from one subsidiary to another subsidiary. If managers need to inflate the performance of a subsidiary one day – perhaps to attract investors – they can transfer capital from another subsidiary. Auditors and other assessors cannot as readily trace these transfers. Hence, financial malfeasance is facilitated.

> ✗ Many organizations are subsidiaries of extensive network of companies. Financial malfeasance, mistrust and job insecurity are slightly more prevalent in these organizations.

The exaggerated upside of downsizing

Some events are unlikely to unfold more than once in the life of a person or organization. For example, husbands are unlikely to ever repeat the answer 'maybe a bit, but I like a bit of fat' to his wife.

Similarly, many people assume that organizations are unlikely to retrench employees more than once in a decade. They believe the rhetoric that organizations, after retrenching unproductive or redundant employees and therefore containing needless costs, will thrive in the future. They know that retrenchments might be tumultuous at the time but, nevertheless, presume the organization will reap the benefits later.

Admittedly, astute employees and managers recognize that retrenchments can provoke a series of complications. They are aware of the obvious expenses: the costs of severance pay, administration and legal advice as well as recruitment and training in the future. They realize that many erudite and skilful employees – employees who have acquired some exclusive and valuable knowledge and insight about the industry – will transfer to rival companies. They expect that job security and morale might decline, at least temporarily, as workload and stress escalates.

For example, several years ago, one company in Sydney announced that over 1,000 people would be retrenched. Employees were stunned and dazed. Days later, however, an accounting firm calculated all the apparent costs, as well as the subtle expenses, of this retrenchment. After this comprehensive analysis, they recognized that expenses would override the savings. The next week, the company decided to abandon this proposal.

Nevertheless, many people often underestimate some of the most pernicious consequences. To illustrate, when organizations donate money to charities or initiate some other altruistic activity, their status tends to escalate. People assume, often unwittingly, that these organizations must be flourishing. They presume these organizations would not be donating time or money unless they were thriving.

In contrast, when organizations withhold donations, and behave uncharitably, people assume these organizations are deteriorating. They presume that marketshare is waning or other problems have transpired.

To illustrate, a man who decides to sell his left arm does not inspire other people with confidence. Even justifications like 'I wasn't really using it anyway' or 'it was in the way whenever I slept on my left side' do not nullify this concern. Similarly, when organizations retrench employees, and thus seem to act uncharitably, they do not inspire confidence in shareholders or potential employees. Their reputation generally declines (Zyglidopoulos 2005). The quality of their products, services and management is assumed to be deficient, and their level of innovation, financial viability and environmental responsibility is perceived as unsatisfactory.

As their reputation wanes, a vast sequence of unforeseen problems often eventuates. Investors transfer their funds to more promising companies. The share price, therefore, tends to decline, sometimes precipitously. Executives are not as likely to receive their expected bonuses. Consequently, they become more likely to consider improper practices. They might attempt to conceal expenses, inflate projections of economic growth and retain unviable activities, primarily to feign confidence and optimism. That is, they reach decisions to appease shareholders rather than improve the organization.

Over time, costs, challenges and complications mount until the problems cannot be concealed any longer, and further retrenchments are thus initiated. Morale plummets, stress soars, and the wellbeing of employees descends. Indeed, many studies indicate that retrenchments at one time increase the likelihood of retrenchments soon afterwards, sometimes within the same year (Cascio 2002).

Second, as their reputation diminishes, organizations cannot as readily attract prospective employees. They cannot attract the most gifted or innovative people. The costs of recruitment and training thus escalate as well.

✖ Sometimes, organizations retrench many employees, perhaps more than five percent of the workforce, during a year. This information is often specified in annual reports or other documents. If more than five percent of the workforce had been retrenched during the last year, the work environment is often demanding and unpredictable.

The exorbitance of executives

Even during the midst of retrenchments and other complications, the salaries and bonuses of executives are often excessive. Most annual reports will specify the remuneration of executives, including their salary and bonuses. Exorbitant levels of pay coincide with a raft of complications.

For example, employees often assume these executives are not dedicated to the welfare of this company (Miller & Wiseman 2001). They feel these executives are motivated by greed – and by greed alone. Employees do not feel their needs and concerns will be accommodated. This assumption provokes a host of problems: cooperation dissipates, innovation diminishes, and the organization declines.

Furthermore, when executive pay is exorbitant, the organization is especially hierarchical. To justify their salaries, these executives are granted unmitigated power and influence. Employees are not granted as many opportunities to participate in decisions. Leaders tends to be autocratic instead of shared. Unforeseen demands are often imposed; anxiety and pressure are rife.

Despite these problems, executives often deride any decreases to their packages. Some executives insist they need these exorbitant salaries, often exceeding $5 million a year excluding bonuses, to maintain their lifestyles. They need this money to service their mortgages, debts and other expenses. Unlike everyone else, these executives seem unable to subsist on 100 times the average salary. Although assigned the role to manage the finances of their company, these managers cannot even manage their personal expenses.

✔ In some organizations, executive remuneration is not as competitive as rival companies that are similar in size. Annual salary, together with bonuses, is less than $1 million for every manager, including the CEO. These organizations are not usually as hierarchical. Managers and employees are more likely to cooperate with each other. Individuals are not as likely to be subjected to unexpected demands.

In addition to their salary, in many companies CEOs and sometimes other executives receive enormous bonuses. Indeed, in many instances a significant portion, sometimes more than half, of the money that CEOs earn is derived from bonuses.

For example, many CEOs are offered stock options – the right to purchase shares at a specific price. To illustrate, the share price might be $1 now. They might be offered the right to purchase 100,000 shares for $1 in one year. If the share price increases to $2 over this time, this 100,000 shares is worth $200,000 but costs only $100,000. If the share price increases to $4 over this time, this 100,000 shares is worth $400,000 but still costs them only $100,000.

In short, if the share price escalates, these stock options are especially attractive. The CEO, therefore, feels inspired to increase the share price of the company. They could, for example, promulgate an inspiring vision, streamline the operations, or initiative other innovative endeavors to pursue this goal.

This scheme, therefore, is intended to motivate CEOs. In one sense, this goal is often fulfilled: CEOs are, at least, often motivated to perpetrate fraud. That is, CEOs will sometimes inflate the projected revenue, or underestimate the likely expenses, to increase the share price, which leads to them misrepresenting the financial position of the organization.

Nevertheless, CEOs do not always commit fraud in these circumstances. That is, in some instances the board of directors, carefully and adeptly, monitors the finances and operations of the organization. These directors are more likely to uncover fraud or other irregularities. Consequently, the benefits of fraud no longer overshadow the risks. CEOs are instead more inclined to enhance the organization than to misrepresent performance. They are more likely to introduce legitimate improvements than to consider illegitimate activities.

Somehow, job applicants need to ascertain whether the board of directors monitors the organization diligently and vigilantly. To illustrate, job applicants should, if possible, determine whether or not the directors also receive sizeable bonuses, including stock options. As research has verified, if the directors also receive sizeable bonuses, they are not as motivated to monitor the organization (O'Connor Jr *et al.* 2006).

That is, in these instances, directors benefit from misleading financial statements, at least initially. If fraud is committed and the share price is inflated, these directors are also more likely to receive sizeable bonuses, and they are not as inclined to prevent fraud. The finances are often misrepresented.

> **✖** In some companies, a significant portion of the money that directors receive – sometimes more than 25 percent – is derived from bonuses like stock options. In these organizations, fraud is more common, and mistrust and job insecurity often pervade the culture.

Positive, but not plausible, thinking

In modern society, optimism is cherished. A positive outlook is regarded as a key virtue. Managers prefer optimistic to pessimistic individuals. They want to believe the organization is thriving, increasing the value of their stock options. They will, therefore, gravitate towards anyone who communicates optimism. They want their employees to perceive the proverbial glass as half full rather than half empty.

Curiously, if individuals direct their attention to the bottom half of the glass, this vessel would seem quite full. Conversely, if they direct their attention to the top half, the glass seems quite empty. Therefore, according to this literal interpretation, people who perceive the glass as more full than empty direct their attention to the bottom half. Interestingly, as research indicates, when individuals orient their attention to the bottom, rather than top, half of space, they are more likely to experience negative emotions.

For example, unpleasant concepts that appear towards the bottom of a computer monitor are recognized swiftly. Unpleasant concepts that appear towards the top of a computer monitor are sometimes overlooked (Meier & Robinson 2006). The bottom half of physical space is associated with adversity and dejection. According to this reasoning, individuals who maintain the glass is half full actually experience more negative states and emotions.

Although merely a metaphor, recent studies also indicate that undue optimism in organizations also coincides with many adverse experiences. As research shows, optimistic forecasts in annual reports often provoke duplicitous, illicit and unethical practices (Prechel & Morris 2010). Managers soon realize they cannot fulfil these forecasts. They begin to panic, seeking any opportunity they can to enhance workplace performance and preserve their reputation. They manipulate their accounts and initiate other expedient measures.

After a while, however, the reality prevails. On one day, employees assume the organization is thriving. The next day, they discover their perceptions have been misguided, and jobs need to be terminated. The environment seems unpredictable and unstable.

> ✗ In some annual reports or other documents, the managers forecast an increase of more than a 25 percent in profit, revenue or sales. These organizations tend to be more unpredictable; job insecurity is common.

Where Should I Work?

Part D

Observations During Interviews
with Supervisors or Managers

Chapter 10

Physical features of your immediate supervisor

You expected you will be interviewer by a man with a deep voice, a strong presence, and a masculine style. However, the appearance and style of the manager diverged considerably from your expectations. He was thinner than you had predicted, with blue eyes and small hands, but long index fingers. During the interview, he sat on the other side of a long table, so far away that you could not hear all of his words. Only one of these features was slightly disconcerting...

Sometimes, you will be able to observe the supervisor or manager before your interview. A video of this person might appear on the internet, perhaps on facebook or YouTube. On other occasions, you might not meet this individual until the interview. Although uncommon, in some instances, you will not even meet your supervisor or manager until after you begin the job – an unsatisfactory circumstance, given that this person is integral to your experience at work.

Admittedly, the behaviour of supervisors and managers during an interview might deviate from their conduct in the workplace. Nevertheless, some of their physical features, including their appearance and mannerisms, can be edifying, indicating whether or not they are likely to be supportive and understanding rather than harsh and unsympathetic.

Every man for himself

Several years ago, a manager was slowly recovering from a chest cold. One day, while darting down the street, he spotted two clients he had not seen during the last year. In his haste, he shouted: 'Give my regards to your wife and kids'. Unfortunately, because of his cough, his voice was hoarse like a mafia boss. Therefore, his reference to their wife and kids sounded like a veiled threat. The clients were aghast but, during the next day, dutifully visited his shop and bought many items.

People often misconstrue the intentions of another person. Nevertheless, some important insights can be distilled from the voice of managers and supervisors. For example, in general, managers with a very deep voice, especially if male, are more likely to be aggressive and violent – or even perpetrate crimes (Ellis, Das & Buker 2008).

To illustrate, according to previous research, elevated levels of testosterone tend to coincide with violent, competitive and aggressive behaviour. That is, testosterone initiates activity in the brain that can evoke competitive and risky inclinations, sometimes culminating in violent or criminal acts.

Therefore, to determine whether your manager is likely to be aggressive and competitive instead of supportive and cooperative, you need to gauge their levels of testosterone. Assuming that you cannot persuade these individuals to urinate in a jar during the interview , you will need to consider other sources of information.

Fortunately, a deep voice signifies elevated levels of testosterone. Similarly, other masculine features, such as a hairy or muscular body, also tends to indicate significant testosterone. Research has indeed confirmed that indices of testosterone – such as a deep voice or a hairy body – do predict the incidence of criminal behaviour (Ellis, Das & Buker 2008).

Interestingly, managers with masculine features, especially if male, are not only often more aggressive themselves, but also tend to evoke a competitive mindset in other people. For instance, when employees interact with someone who speaks in a deep, booming voice, they become more competitive themselves. They are not as inclined to trust these people (Miller, Maner & Becker 2010). Therefore, if the managers tend to be very masculine in style, a competitive rather than cooperative culture is likely to permeate the organization.

One Australian company epitomizes this ruthless culture. This company offers plumbing and electrical services to households. Whenever customers arrange an appointment with a representative of this company, their details, including their address as well as the scheduled time and date, are recorded in a spreadsheet. One day, to undermine his colleagues, one employee, called John, sent a brochure to every customer who had arranged one of these appointments. The brochure indicated this company is an unlawful organization. If customers are contacted by this organization, they should telephone another number. When they telephoned this number, a woman would answer and would recommend John instead – whom unbeknownst to the customers was actually her husband. Until he was caught, John attracted more sales than any other employee in the history of this company.

> ✖ Sometimes, during interviews, the managers seem very masculine in style. For example, their voice is deep, their physique is robust, and their body is hairy. These managers, especially if male, are not as likely to be supportive and cooperative, or to foster a collaborative environment.

Palm snake oil

Subtle features of the hands can also indicate a masculine, competitive demeanour. Few people, however, are attuned to these features.

Admittedly, some job applicants attempt to derive information from reading the palms of their prospective managers. They might, for example, examine the head line – the bottom of the two horizontal creases that cross the palm – to establish whether or not the manager is receptive to creativity. They might check the girdle of Venus, originating in the space between the ring and little fingers, to establish the emotional intelligence of individuals. Finally, they might scan the sun line, under the ring finger, to ascertain whether or not the person will be involved in a scandal.

This approach could be informative, apart from two minor concerns. First, when requested to reveal their palms, managers may not comply. They will respond to this request, but usually by telephoning security.

Second, palm reading may be complete hogwash. At least, no scientific research has established an association between the lines and characteristics of palms and the personalities of individuals.

Nevertheless, one approach that, at first glance, resembles palm reading has actually been vindicated scientifically. Specifically, the relative length of the index and ring fingers – usually called the digit ratio – does, actually, correlate with personality. In particular, in most individuals the ring finger is slightly longer than is the index finger, on both hands. Nevertheless, in some people, the ring finger is considerably longer, perhaps by 1.5 cm or more. In other people, the ring finger is almost as short, if not shorter, than is the index finger.

Interestingly, the relative length of these fingers depends on prenatal testosterone – that is, levels of testosterone in the blood before birth. Elevated levels of testosterone, for some reason, reduce the relative length of the index finger. Therefore, a short index finger, compared to the ring finger, indicates that testosterone levels were pronounced before birth.

Furthermore, these testosterone levels tend to correlate with masculine traits later in life. When prenatal testosterone levels are elevated and the index finger is short, individuals tend to be more aggressive later in life. They enjoy competition and achievement more than collaboration and cooperation, and they seek positions of power and influence.

Similarly, when prenatal testosterone levels are elevated, individuals will tend to neglect emotions later in life. They will not, for example, share their feelings with friends. They will not be especially sensitive to the emotional needs of other people.

An appalling irony thus evolves. People with short index fingers are willing to compete vigorously to secure a position of power. They will, therefore, dominate leadership positions. However, because they are competitive but insensitive, they do not cultivate a supportive, cohesive environment. They do not encourage employees to share their feelings and develop trust, and they do not foster a culture that, ultimately, facilitates wellbeing.

Many studies have confirmed that digit ratio is indeed associated with personality. One study, for example, showed that short index fingers, relative to ring fingers, coincide with traits that are related to testosterone. Individuals with short index fingers tend to seek competition, feel tough, and neglect emotions (Fisher *et al.* 2010). They are not as likely to share their feelings with friends, enjoy intimacy, or trust their intuition.

> ✓ Sometimes, during meeting, managers place their palms on the table. If their index finger is long – as long as, if not longer than, their ring finger – they are more likely to be collaborative, sensitive and understanding.

Beaten brown and blue

If managers do not parade their hands, you can instead consider a more conspicuous feature: their eyes. The eyes of some people are particularly narrow – significantly narrower than other individuals of their ethnicity. In general, individuals are not as likely to trust people with unexpectedly narrow eyes.

As research shows, whenever someone with unexpectedly narrow eyes utters a word or phrase, the other individuals will consider the antonym of this expression (Schul, Mayo &

Burnstein 2004). If this suspicious person, for example, expresses the phrase 'this food is tasty', other individuals form a mental image of bland or unappetizing food. If this person utters the word 'white', other individuals imagine a black object instead. This inclination most likely evolved to ensure that individuals are not misled by nefarious people.

However, as other research has shown, the colour of eyes, and not the shape, often indicates whether a manager is likely to be dominating or cooperative. Men with brown eyes in particular tend to be more dominating and forceful rather than cooperative and accommodating (Kleisner *et al.* 2010). Men with blue eyes, however, tend to be more supportive and obliging.

One possible rejoinder is that men with brown eyes are not actually more dominating – perhaps other people merely assume these men are more dominating. Hence, individuals often perceive these men as forceful or aggressive, regardless of their actual behaviour. Yet this explanation has been invalidated. Specifically, if men with brown eyes wear blue contact lenses, modifying the perceived colour of their eyes, they still tend to be perceived as more dominating.

> ✓ Occasionally, the eye colour of a male manager or supervisor is blue. This manager is likely to be more supportive and cooperative than male managers or supervisors with brown eyes.

Sit by me

In addition to the innate features of managers, the physical mannerisms of these individuals are also revealing. The seating arrangement during job interviews, for example, is particularly informative. Sometimes, the manager will sit close to you, within a meter or two. On other occasions, the manager might sit farther away, perhaps at the other end of a long table.

If managers do sit far away, you should perhaps be concerned. Either someone has inadvertently swapped your underarm deodorant with fly spray, or this manager is not especially cooperative and supportive. That is, as research shows, if individuals experience a sense of connection and bond to other people, often translating into cooperation and trust, they prefer to sit relative close to someone else in the room (Holland *et al.* 2004).

However, if individuals feel disconnected and detached, they will prefer to sit farther away. These people are often more competitive than cooperative. They are seldom understanding or sensitive.

For example, at a retail store in Toronto, one manager was renowned for his insensitive outbursts. The son of one of his employees had recently been killed by a speeding motorist, drag racing in the suburban street. Nevertheless, every day, she would dutifully arrive at work. Occasionally, however, she would burst into tears and would need to leave the premises for several minutes. Every time she returned, the manager would castigate her vehemently, demanding that she remain in the shop at all times during work hours.

One day, she decided she could no longer work and resigned in tears. The manager experienced a moment of guilt. He decided, perhaps for the first time in his career, to buy her a parting gift. Unfortunately, he gift was not entirely appropriate: he presented her with two tickets to the Grand Prix.

> ✓ Sometimes, during an interview, the managers or supervisors sit close to you, within one or two meters from your chair. These managers and supervisors are often supportive and understanding, and motivated to resolve conflicts.

Milking chocolate

Some people do not know how to eat chocolate. Although usually aware of which orifice into which the chocolate should be inserted, they do not know how to savor the experience.

They do not, for example, chew slowly and deliberately, orienting their attention to the texture and taste of this delicacy. They remain oblivious to the variety of sensations that chocolates evoke as they gradually dissolve in the mouth.

Apart from chocolate, these individuals might also not be able to savor quiet, positive experiences in general: stimulating conversations, summer breezes, or delightful music, for example. These experiences, rather than appreciated, are consumed perfunctorily and swiftly, like a chore that needs to be completed.

This reluctance to savor, obviously, diminishes the intensity of positive experiences but also reflects other concerns. In particular, this reluctance can sometimes indicate the person is unkind, uncaring and uncooperative.

To demonstrate, if the right hemisphere of the brain is especially active, people are more inclined to seek and to maintain strong, fulfilling relationships (Kuhl & Kazen 2008). To fulfill this need, these individuals are more sensitive to the needs and concerns of other people. Because of this concern, they are more attuned to emotions. They recognize and understand the feeling of other people. They also appreciate their own emotional experiences.

If the left hemisphere of the brain is particularly active instead, people are more inclined to establish and to enhance their wealth, power and status. They often neglect the needs and concerns of other people. They are not as attuned to emotions and sensations, either in themselves or in other individuals. Therefore, they are not as inclined to relish, appreciate or savor their positive experiences.

Research has corroborated these proposals (Quoidbach *et al.* 2010). For example, wealthy individuals are not as likely to savor positive experiences. They do not undertake the activities that prolong or amplify positive emotions, such as maintain their concentration on a pleasing scene like a waterfall or describe this event to other people.

Similarly, even when individuals are merely exposed to photographs of money, they are subsequently not as inclined to savor these experiences. They tend to swallow chocolates quickly, often without awareness. Thus, money, wealth and power – all of which often deter care and cooperation – are not associated with attempts to savor experiences (Quoidbach *et al.* 2010).

Therefore, during interviews, you should gauge whether the managers savor positive experiences. Do they drink their coffee or consume a sweet gradually and deliberately? Do they relish in other tranquil, enjoyable experiences, like briefly observing the trees outside? Do they mention their penchant for other soothing experiences, like yoga?

✓ Some managers seem to savor positive, soothing experiences. They might consume food slowly or enjoy other tranquil events. These managers tend to be supportive and understanding instead of competitive or domineering.

Chapter 11

Hints of deception and dishonesty

During the interview, the manager regales you with some delightful anecdotes about the organization: eccentric but supportive managers, remarkable achievements, and some exciting opportunities. Nevertheless, as the manager continues, you wonder whether or not these accounts are accurate. You are not certain whether the manager has concealed some key details or disconcerting problems. Admittedly, the accounts were vivid. The manager had spoken with enthusiasm, gesticulating passionately with both arms, staring intensely, but then blinking rapidly after completing his tale. Although buoyed by these anecdotes, one of these behaviours evokes suspicion...

At the Academy Awards, after prevailing in the category for best male or female actor, most recipients attempt to feign humility. They might, for example, declare they feel so humbled to be mentioned alongside the other great artists in this category. They might voice the honor they feel to win this exalted award. Most of the audience, however, do not seem to recognize the irony that a person can win the category for best male or female actor but seem so unconvincing when they attempt to feign humility.

In contrast to these Hollywood actors, some managers are able to feign humility, honesty and integrity very well. During interviews and discussions, managers, supervisors, and even potential colleagues will sometimes convey inaccurate information. These individuals do not want applicants, especially promising applicants, to reject job offers.

Consequently, managers might trivialize or conceal some of the problems in the organization: the unbridled workload, the obsolete equipment, or the volatile executives, for example. Supervisors might feign a supportive, sympathetic manner, vaguely aware they tend to be uncompromising and forceful at work. Potential colleagues might seem content and satisfied, while concealing their intention to leave the company as swiftly as possible.

In general, the cues that indicate deception are seldom, if ever, especially conspicuous. You are unlikely, for example, to be able to attach a polygraph to these individuals, despite persuasive observations like 'You know, I think you would look really good with this sticker attached to your chest.'

Fortunately, after hundreds of studies into the cues that coincide with deception, scientists have uncovered some helpful principles. As these studies demonstrate, blinking patterns in the eyes, movements of the hands or fingers, references to specific details, duration of answers and errors during speech can sometimes be scrutinized to differentiate accurate from contrived answers.

I do not believe your eyes

Although job applicants might want to ascertain whether the manager or recruiter is lying or exaggerating, they do not want to appear unusual. For example, if applicants are informed they should count the number of times the person shifts their hips, they might appear somewhat odd as they fix their eyes on the crotch of this manager.

Fortunately, some of the methods that people can use to determine whether someone is lying or exaggerating are seamless rather than unnatural. Specifically, many studies indicate the job applicants should direct their attention to the facial expressions of the other person.

When individuals are sensitive to movements, such as fleeting changes in the facial expression of people, they are naturally more likely to detect instances of probable deception. Their conjectures about whether someone is lying or not are more likely to be accurate (Warren, Schertler & Bull 2010). Given that one of the investigators of this study is called Dr Bull, these scholars are probably especially attuned to this topic.

One facial movement is particularly telling: the rate of blinking. While individuals concoct an event, the rate of blinking tends to diminish. Sometimes, their eyes do not even blink at all but remain open. Immediately afterwards, however, the rate of blinking tends to increase (Leal & Vrij 2008).

Admittedly, many other changes in the eyes also correlate with lying. When people fabricate an account, their pupils often dilate (DePaulo *et al.* 2003). This dilation could be ascribed to anxiety and arousal, or to concentration and attention. Nevertheless, unless you are peering uncomfortably into the eyes of this person, this dilation is difficult to detect.

> ✖ During interviews, managers or supervisors will often describe positive features of the work environment. They might contend the workplace is supportive and progressive, for example. Before the interview, you could form the intention to peer briefly at the face and eyes of these managers while they extol the virtues of this company. If their eyes do not blink at all during this account, but then blink rapidly immediately afterwards, their depiction of the workplace might have been contrived.

Holding hands

Lie detectors, also called polygraphs, are often used to ascertain whether or not people are truthful. In one sense, lie detectors can be used to identify a liar: anyone who maintains that lie detectors are always effective is a liar. Unfortunately, no tangible cues or physiological indices invariably coincide with lies.

Nevertheless, besides the eyes, the hands and fingers of individuals can also be informative, at least in some instances. Dishonest managers, for example, will tend to stifle their hand and finger movements. That is, the frequency and magnitude of their gestures will diminish.

Specifically, when individuals lie, they often experience an entrenched inclination to inhibit any signals that could reveal their dishonesty. They will, therefore, suppress any needless movements. Their hands in particular are more likely to be still (Vrij, Akehurst & Morris 1997).

> ✖ Before the interview, you should form the intention to peer briefly at the hands and fingers of the managers while they extol the virtues of this company. If their hands and fingers are especially still during these tributes to the organization, their depiction of the workplace might be inaccurate. Nevertheless, some categories of hand and finger movements are actually more prevalent while individuals lie (Caso et al. 2006); hand and finger movement, therefore, do not necessarily indicate that managers are sincere.

No time to lose

In addition to the mannerisms, the words of individuals can also be telling. When people contrive or concoct some event – for example, when they describe some achievement that did not actually transpire – they seldom refer to time (Sporer & Sharman 2006).

While they lie, individuals will seldom, if ever, mention the time of day, such as 'in the afternoon, I decided to help the employees'. They will also not refer to the day, like 'a few Fridays ago, we had a great time developing this idea'. In addition, they are also unlikely to allude to the time of year, such as the month or season.

That is, when managers contrive or inflate some event, their attention is fixated on the main sequence of events. They do not consider the time of day or year. Indeed, they do not contemplate the surrounding context at all.

Indeed, concocted or exaggerated accounts seldom refer to other details in the context: the sights, sounds, and smells in the environment (Vrij, Edward & Bull 2001). If people fabricate some event, they will not often allude to incidental features like 'we were standing near a white gate', 'it was quiet', or 'it smelt like the sea', unless these features are integral to the anecdote.

> ✓ After an interview, you could attempt to remember the times in which the managers extolled the virtues of this organization. Specifically, you should recall a description of a particular event or project, intended to demonstrate the merits of this workplace. If the managers referred to specific times, days or seasons – or alluded to incidental details like the color of objects or the sounds in the environment – their account was probably accurate.

Short descriptions of tall tales

When individuals lie, not only do they seldom allude to incidental details, their answers and accounts tend to be short (Sporer & Schwandt 2006). They attempt to finish their sentence as rapidly as possible. They may feel, on some level, that brief accounts are not as likely to be challenged. Brief accounts reduce the likelihood that perhaps their deception will be exposed.

For example, one IT company, located in Bangalore, wanted to engage the services of an expert in lie detection. They needed to determine which of their employees had stolen goods. The company, therefore, advertised this position in the local newspaper.

The next day, a person who had acquired no expertise in this field applied. This person knew that he would be able to convince the company that he was proficient: after all, he knew that nobody at the organization is trained to identify lies, because otherwise they would not have advertised this position. He merely presented a short account of his expertise – 'I worked ten years in intelligence' – and was awarded the role within minutes.

Nevertheless, despite this brevity, when individuals fabricate these accounts, they are more likely to repeat themselves (DePaulo *et al.* 2003). They might, for example, repeat the same word or phrase in rapid succession. Alternatively, they might emphasize the same detail or premise twice, unnecessarily.

> ✓ After an interview, you could attempt to remember the times in which the managers extolled the virtues of this organization. If these answers or accounts were very short – or included repetition of particular phrases or details – their depiction of the workplace might have been inaccurate.

...Um

Furthermore, when people concoct an account, they are more likely to commit speech errors. They are, for example, more likely to emit hesitations, such as 'ums,' 'ers,' and 'ahs.' They are also not as likely to complete sentences, like 'the customers were really happy with...'. In addition, they might stutter or utter the wrong word – a word that is not applicable to the sentence (DePaulo *et al.* 2003).

Despite these errors, whenever individuals lie, they are not as inclined to concede mistakes (DePaulo *et al.* 2003). As they lie, their willingness to retract a remark diminishes. They will seldom amend a detail, with words like 'actually, there was probably only five people rather than ten people'. When asked direct questions, they will not admit they cannot remember the details. Unlike people who describe a genuine account, people who describe a fabricated account will not concede that some of the details are hazy.

> ✓ After an interview, you could attempt to remember the times in which the managers extolled the virtues of this organization. If the managers corrected some of their previous remarks or conceded that some of the details are hazy, their account was probably accurate.

Opportunities and obstacles to uncovering deception

Unfortunately, after individuals are apprised of the subtle cues that indicate deception, their capacity to decide whether someone is lying or not does not always improve. That is, these individuals will attempt to apply the insights they have acquired. They will deliberate carefully. Contrary to depictions on TV, research has shown that considered deliberations will tend to impair, rather than enhance, their capacity to identify lies.

For example, in one study, some participants watched an extended conversation. The other participants watched only fleeting slices of this conversation. Their task was to identify whether or not specific remarks were true or false. In general, if participants watched only fleeting slices, rather than entire conversations, they could more readily distinguish between true and false statements (Albrechtsen, Meissner & Susa 2009).

In particular, if the conversation is extensive, individuals deliberate on many features and cues to assess the veracity of these comments. They might notice the comments are inconsistent with each other and the person often gesticulates with both hands. Nevertheless, assumptions about which of these cues indicate deception are often misguided. Some people, for example, might incorrectly presume that inconsistent statements and frequent gesticulations reflect dishonesty. Their deliberations, therefore, frequently generate unfounded conclusions.

Furthermore, when individuals deliberate on some cues, they may overlook other sources of information. They may neglect other telling hints.

In contrast, when people only observe fleeting slices of an extended conversation, they cannot analyze these cues as explicitly and deliberately. To some extent, they often need to utilize their intuition or hunches. These intuitions often integrate an extensive range of informative cues: vocal characteristics, hand movements, facial expressions, and word usage, for example. Signs of dishonesty are often detected, usually unconsciously. True and false statements can be distinguished, at least occasionally

In some conditions, these intuitions are especially astute. Interestingly, when individuals communicate with someone who is closer to their left shoulder than to their right shoulder, their intuition is usually more accurate. They can more readily decipher the emotions, intentions, or motives of a person who is nearer to their left side (Puccinelli, Tickle-Degnen & Rosenthal 2004). They can, for example, determine whether a manager is deceptive or sincere.

Crashing after a crash course

Because careful deliberation is not always effective, workbooks and workshops on how individuals can identify deception are sometimes futile. For example, in one study, police officers, social workers and students all participated in a training program intended to enhance their ability to detect dishonesty. They were exposed to a specific approach, called the Criteria Based Content Analysis. Specifically, they were informed about the words and sentences that often reflect deception. They were told, for example, that individuals seldom describe the context or surroundings, reproduce specific quotes, allude to unusual or superfluous details, refer to their own mental state, or admit to uncertainty or errors when they lie.

This training, however, did not assist all of these participants Akehurst, Bull, Vrij & Köhnken 2004). Indeed, after the training, the capacity of police officers to identify deception actually declined. That is, they were not as able as previously to distinguish between true and false written testimonies.

Instead, to identify dishonesty during interviews, you should complete a series of five phases. First, a night or so before the interview, you should form an image in your mind of the cues that indicate deception. You could envisage the managers blinking only after, but not while, they describe the organization. You could imagine these individuals speaking while their hands or fingers remain almost unnaturally still. You could envisage an account of events that is devoid of any references to the time or the surroundings but replete with repetitions or errors.

Second, after you form these images, you could repeat to yourself something like 'if the managers blinks only after, but not while, they speak, consider that perhaps their accounts of the organization are distorted'. You could repeat this sentence for each cue. You do not need to memorize these principles. Instead, after you form these images and repeat these statements, your attention will effortlessly, but only momentarily, shift to the relevant mannerisms and behaviours (Adriaanse, de Ridder & de Wit 2009). You will intuit any deception, while otherwise maintaining your concentration on the interview.

Third, if possible, during the interview, ensure your left shoulder, rather than right shoulder, is closer to the manager. Fourth, after the interview, you should review all the mannerisms of these managers as well as their questions and answers. Consider all the cues that indicate deception. Can you remember the rate of their blinking, the movement of their arms or fingers, or the errors in their speech? Can you remember whether or not they alluded to details about the time and surroundings?

Finally, after a period of distraction – perhaps an hour or so – trust your intuition. Do you feel the manager was sincere? Is your hunch that perhaps the manager was truthful?

Chapter 12

The language of your immediate supervisor

From the outset, the manager seemed friendly and amicable. 'I feel delighted to meet you', he said as he began the interview. After asking some question, he then described all the remarkable initiatives, achievements, and characteristics of the company: the excellent rapport between managers and employees, the customer service awards, and the innovative procedures. He mentioned that all of these procedures were introduced to help employees reach their personal goals. The manager enumerated some of these procedures on a piece of paper, rotated the paper to ensure you could read the contents, and then, after a few moments, continued with a few more questions. You feel inspired, apart from one impediment .

During interviews, you should listen carefully to the words or phrases the manager articulates – not because these words or phrases are especially insightful, but merely because the precise language can be illuminating. The words that your immediate supervisor or manager expresses, especially towards the end of an interview after the formal questions have been asked, can impart some key information about the temperament of these individuals and the culture or climate of the work environment.

Trust me

Managers are not usually as cooperative and moral as they pretend to be. Most, but not all, managers and supervisors will attempt to portray themselves as supportive, cooperative, and moral. They might contend they are helpful and constructive as well as just and fair. However, many individuals are not as moral as they believe.

One illuminating set of studies demonstrates this complication. In these studies, the participants are told that two activities need to be completed. Both tasks comprise a series of questions that need to be answered. One of these activities, however, is desirable: if they answer a question correctly, the individuals earn a raffle ticket, increasing the likelihood they will win a large prize later. The other activity is undesirable: no raffle tickets are awarded.

The next instruction is significant. Participants are told to assign one of these tasks to themselves and the other tasks to another person – a person who is a stranger and believes the activities have been allocated randomly. Therefore, participants must decide whether to be immoral, and merely assign themselves the desirable task, or moral, and thus apply some other rationale.

Approximately 90 percent of participants conceded that merely allocating themselves the desirable activity would not be moral. Nevertheless, about 75 percent of people did assign this preferred task to themselves. Many of these participants, therefore, did not fulfil their own moral standards.

In a slight variation of this paradigm, some participants are invited to toss a coin, perhaps to guide their decision. Surprisingly, over 85 percent of the people who tossed the coin still assigned themselves the desirable task. They tossed the coin, perhaps to seem fair, but actually behaved selfishly anyway (Batson *et al.* 2010).

So, you might be tempted, during job interviews, to believe managers who depict themselves as cooperative and supportive. Unfortunately, the behaviour of individuals does not always accord with the morals they advocate.

Can you feel it?

The words that managers often use can also be telling. Obviously, managers who frequently bellow phrases like 'that utter goose', 'that complete turkey' or 'that birdbrain' are either particularly derogatory, or perhaps avid bird watchers. However, even when managers attempt to seem gracious and welcoming, some of the words they express can, inadvertently, manifest an insensitive demeanor. In contrast, other words manifest sympathy and understanding.

To illustrate, some managers often begin sentences with the phrase 'I think'. They might say 'I think this job would be right for you' or 'I think the market will improve next year'.

Other managers, at least occasionally, begin sentences with the phrase 'I feel'. They could say 'I feel this job would be right for you' or 'I feel the market will improve next year'.

In general, if managers usually orient their attention to objective facts rather than subjective feelings, they are more inclined to begin sentence with the phrase 'I think' rather than 'I feel'. The phrase 'I feel' does not resonate with these individuals. They are, thus, not as likely to express this phrase.

Actually, as scientific analyses have shown, individuals who are more concerned with facts than feelings are seldom persuaded by sentences that begin with the phrase 'I feel'. They tend to disregard these sentences altogether (Mayer & Tormala 2010).

One of these managers, for example, previously a distinguished engineer, was listening to a distraught employee on day. Her daughter had recently been diagnosed with a fatal bone disorder. The employee sought leave, for only one week, to travel to America and visit a renowned specialist. While she related the pain and suffering of her daughter and the plethora of failed interventions, she cried genuinely and uncontrollably. The manager initially refused the request until, later, he discovered that her insurance company would cover 20 percent of her pay. He was very sensitive to incidental facts, the money, but insensitive to intense emotions.

In contrast, if managers tend to orient their attention to subjective feelings rather than objective facts, they often express the phrase 'I feel'. Therefore, managers who utilize this phrase are more attuned to the feelings and emotions of people. They sympathize with employees who feel upset. They accommodate individuals who seem anxious. They embrace initiatives that fulfill the needs and enhance the emotions of employees. These managers, therefore, are more likely to cultivate a supportive, cooperative environment – an environment that appreciates people and wellbeing rather than merely success and money.

✓ During some interviews, the manager, at least occasionally, refers to the word 'feel' or 'feeling'. Furthermore, the manager often alludes to the importance of subjective experiences like passion and excitement, rather than tangible rewards such as money or promotions. These managers will tend to be sympathetic and supportive in the workplace.

Can they handle the truth

In addition to the words, the sentiments of managers also reflect their style. When companies announce a liquidation sale, they always seem very excited during the advertisements. They often shout, in a frenzied, energized, and excited voice, that all stock must be sold at ridiculous prices. However, given the company is forced to shut the business and sell their stock at negligible prices, they should probably feel depressed rather than excited. In these commercials, the announcer should be crying, pleading with customers to purchase these unwanted products and asking whether or not anyone knows of any vacant positions.

Some employees and managers also attempt to seem upbeat and optimistic, even in trying circumstances. They seldom allude to problems, complications, obstacles or challenges. Instead, they always orient their attention to the opportunities or benefits of some event. If redundancies are imminent, they may contend that only the best people will remain and the organization will thrive. If the salaries of employees are slashed, they may argue the work environment will be more supportive in the future, offsetting this decline in pay.

For some people, this positive demeanor is effortless and genuine. They naturally and sincerely feel optimistic and hopeful. For other people, this positive demeanor is feigned and contrived. They feel the need, if not the obligation, to seem upbeat and cheerful.

If managers feel this need to feign optimism and suppress doubt, two important problems can unfold. First, these managers tend to be moody and unpredictable. That is, they attempt to suppress or inhibit negative thoughts, emotions or appraisals. They strive to distract themselves from doubts, concerns and anxieties.

Attempts to suppress unpleasant thoughts or emotions are usually effective, but only initially. After a few minutes or hours, doubts, concerns and anxieties are typically reinstated, usually more intensely than before (e.g. Borton, Markovitz & Dieterich 2005). These managers, therefore, will sometimes seem cheerful, supportive and buoyant at one time, and then, perhaps an hour or so later, they might be enraged, distraught, frantic or tense. Their mood is inexplicably erratic; their behaviour is unpredictable.

Furthermore, because their mood varies appreciably across the day or week, these managers often modify their decisions unexpectedly. When they seem content or satisfied, they are more inclined to support more ambitious projects and philanthropic ventures. When anxious or agitated, however, these managers are more likely to dismiss these ambitious or philanthropic endeavors, orienting their attention to the more immediate and pressing needs of the organization. The roles and responsibilities of employees, therefore, will often change intermittently, compromising their progress and wellbeing.

A second problem can transpire whenever managers feel the need to feign optimism and suppress doubt. During job interviews, their attempted depiction of the work environment is typically inaccurate. They do not allude to the complications of this environment: the excessive workload, the limited autonomy, the competition between departments, the autocratic management, the inadequate training, the contempt towards innovation, or the scarcity of feedback, for example. That is, they do not convey a realistic preview of the impending job.

Many studies have shown that such distorted previews compromise job satisfaction. Specific problems, such as excessive work demands, are not as consequential when anticipated (Buckley *et al.* 2002).

During the job interview, you cannot ascertain whether or not the job preview is actually unbiased. You can, however, determine whether or not the manager is willing to concede obstacles, complications and problems rather than suppress these challenges. That is, managers might admit to some of the problems that pervade the environment at work, but with a balanced perspective. They might concede that 'sometimes the demands are very heavy, but we are trying to stabilize these workloads' or that 'managers do not always listen to ideas immediately, although this problem has improved'.

> ✓ During some interview, managers seem to offer a balanced account of the work environment. They do concede that some problems are common, but the environment is nevertheless supportive and productive. These organizations are more likely to be stable and predictable, perhaps imparting a sense of control. You are not as likely to feel disappointed or disenchanted in these environments.

Everyone, apart from me, is suspicious

In modern societies, managers often like to depict themselves as firm but fair. By firm, they mean they are susceptible to the occasional pathological tirade, secreting more froth than an overflowing cappuccino machine. By fair, they ... well ... do not really mean anything at all.

Some managers are not firm, resolute, and assertive – they are just plain aggressive. Their outbursts are unjustifiable. Their anger is often uncontrollable.

Their motivation is often to undermine, rather than to help, their employees. And, consistent with this motivation, they do not help their employees. That is, aggressive managers elicit a sense of vigilance in employees – an enduring feeling of apprehension – that disrupts any sense of meaning at work and inhibits wellbeing.

Managers are even more likely to be aggressive than peers. When individuals are assigned to positions of power – team leader, general manager or even board member – they feel an increasing need to demonstrate their competence. They feel, on some level, that they should be capable, talented and accomplished.

Occasionally, managers feel they do not fulfill these lofty standards. Perhaps, they might be challenged by an employee. Perhaps, they might just remember a time in which they committed a grave error.

Regardless of the origin, these doubts elicit the realization they have not fulfilled the qualities that epitomize their role. Because of these doubts, they anticipate, often unconsciously, an impending adversity – perhaps a strident criticism or looming demotion. These expectations often provoke an aggressive demeanor, as individuals strive to protect their position.

Research has affirmed this argument. In one study, participants answered a series of questions. Some of these questions were asked to determine whether or not the individuals sometimes feel incompetent, inept or inadequate at work. Other questions were asked to ascertain the extent to which these individuals behave aggressively. Unsurprisingly, if individuals often feel incompetent, they are more inclined to behave aggressively. However, in participants who had been assigned positions of power and responsibility at work, this incompetence was especially likely to provoke aggression (Fast & Chen 2009).

Nevertheless, in the context of job interviews, this aggression is unlikely to be evoked. Job applicants, therefore, cannot as readily predict whether this manager or supervisor is likely to be aggressive. The person might seem reasonable now, but appear belligerent in the workplace.

Admittedly, many techniques have been developed recently, as well as validated scientifically, to predict whether individuals are likely to behave aggressively. For example, one of these techniques is called a lexical decision task. The individuals sit in front of a computer and are exposed to strings of letters. Some of these strings are words, like FIST or CARPET. The other strings are not legitimate English words, like DOPIN or BATOO. Their task is to press one key, perhaps the Q, if the string of letters represents a legitimate word, and another key, perhaps the P, if the string of letters does not represent a legitimate word.

People who are aggressive rapidly recognize words that relate to violence, hostility or anger, such as FIST. People who are not aggressive do not recognize these words as rapidly (Denzler, Forster & Liberman 2009).

This technique is obviously not applicable in the context of a job interview. However, one technique is more suitable. Specifically, if managers are aggressive, they tend to espouse particular opinions – opinions that ultimately justify their aggression (James *et al.* 2005).

First, they tend to assume the primary motive of social interactions is to establish dominance instead of trust. They frequently allude to hierarchies or chains of command. They might utter remarks like 'I had to show him who was boss'. They often refer to the hostile intent of other people, such as 'they brought in their cronies to intimidate us', remarks that are intended to legitimate their aggressive inclinations.

Second, they often assume that retribution and punishment are not only a suitable, but also a vital, means to maintain harmony. They assume that people and organizations are inherently immoral or dishonest. They believe that other companies strive to pursue their own interests to the detriment of everyone else. Aggression is thus perceived as a legitimate means to prevent immoral behaviour. They might proffer opinions like 'they won't do what you say unless they respect you' or 'they undertake this audit to annoy us'. They believe that companies might 'intentionally sell flawed products to increase the costs of repair'.

> ✖ Occasionally, during a job interview, the managers express opinions that imply they assume their main goal is to establish dominance. They also presume the primary aim of other people is also to maintain dominance rather than to establish trust. These managers are often aggressive instead of supportive.

Not my fault

Cream is thick, white, and almost exclusively fat. The proverb that 'cream rises to the top', therefore, indicates that individuals who scale the corporate hierarchy, at least in many Western economies, tend to be thick, white, and almost exclusively fat.

In practice, this proverb is promulgated to justify, and not to undermine, managers and executives. Specifically, this phrase implies that managers and executives are indeed the best people. Leaders propagate this message to emphasize their superiority. They want to believe their promotions and achievements are warranted rather than fortuitous. They would like to assume their pay and privileges are just and deserved.

Indeed, many other proverbs reinforce this assumption that success implies superiority. 'Bad workers always blame their tools'. Some people are assumed to be imbued with the 'golden touch'. All of these proverbs imply that some people are inherently superior. All of these expressions are intended to justify the prevailing disparities in income and rights across the levels of management.

Managers and executives are also often granted the power to disseminate these expressions. That is, the individuals in positions of power, almost by definition, are offered more opportunities to contribute to public discourse. Usually, only executives contribute to annual reports. Only senior personnel tend to be invited to speak on radio or TV. Only managers are quoted in financial magazines. The phrases that managers and executives like – the expressions that justify their superiority – are especially likely to permeate society.

These expressions provoke two problems. First, when these proverbs abound, injustices often persist. If cream is assumed to rise to the top, people who have not flourished are presumed to be inferior. They are assumed to be fundamentally deficient. Other impediments to their success – rampant prejudice, unfair evaluations, limited opportunities, and many other obstacles – arc neglected. Injustices remain unchecked

Second, when these proverbs are embraced, the environment becomes more competitive. That is, in some organizations employees and managers tend to believe that some people are inherently superior. They adopt the axiom that cream rises to the top. They assume that superior people will eventually prevail. Consequently, they become more inclined to feel their primary goal in their work life – or indeed in their life generally – is to scale this hierarchy. They strive vigorously to compete and prevail. They want to substantiate their superiority. The environment becomes competitive instead of collaborative, spiteful instead of supportive.

A few subtle cues can indicate that a managers believes some people are inherently superior. These cues indicate that the manager feels only some people deserve special privileges – a belief that perpetuates injustice and undermines cooperation.

In particular, these managers ascribe achievements and failures, almost exclusively, to the qualities or deficiencies of individuals (Dambrun et al. 2009), and neglect other events or impediments. If an employee sells many products, these managers would not attribute this achievement to fortuitous events like a recent tax rebate. If an employee arrives late to work, these managers would not impute this tardiness to unforeseen complications, such as cancelled buses or family illness. Events and changes in the context are neglected.

Interestingly, as one study revealed, when students complete a course in psychology, sociology or some other discipline that addresses the societal determinants of individual wellbeing, they are not as likely to assume that some people are inherently superior. They do not feel that some constituencies deserve more privileges. They strive to redress injustice and feel motivated to cooperate with other people (Dambrun *et al.* 2009).

If managers do, however, assume that some people are inherently superior, their questions seldom refer to the context. They will not, for example, ask questions like: 'In what environment do you feel you work more effectively?' or 'What are the qualities of managers that inspire you'. That is, they will not consider whether or not the work environment at this organization resonates with the preferences of applicants. Instead, they assume, although implicitly, that some applicants flourish and other applicants founder in all environments.

> ✓ During the interview, some managers ask questions about the work environment or leadership style that is most likely to inspire you. These managers recognize the context partly affects performance. These individuals are not as likely to be competitive. They are also more willing to redress injustices, imparting a sense of control to employees.

Writing upside down

If you are reading this chapter near a friend or colleague, you might both want to attempt the following experiment. With a pen, highlighter or marker, draw an E on your own forehead.

Some people draw the E from their own perspective. That is, the stem of this E is located on the left side of their forehead. Others, in contrast, draw the E from the perspective of someone else. That is, the stem of this E is located on the right side.

In general, when individuals experience a sense of power and authority, they tend to draw the E from their own perspective (Galinsky *et al.* 2006). Even if they merely imagine one time in which they were granted this authority, they demonstrate this tendency. Because of their power, they do not feel the need to accommodate the perspective or needs of anyone else. They are not concerned that, to an observer, the pattern resembles the mirror image of an E.

In contrast, when individuals do not experience this sense of power or authority, they draw the E from the perspective of someone else. That is, because their power is limited and hence they feel vulnerable, they attempt to accommodate the needs of other people. They will, therefore, ensure the pattern resembles an E to an observer.

Therefore, when managers feel powerful, they will often neglect the perspective of other people, particularly employees. They might convey feedback that is hurtful or offensive. They might offer incomprehensible instructions, failing to consider the experience or knowledge of the listener. Their employees perennially feel uneasy and uncertain.

Nevertheless, if the manager also experiences a genuine motivation to help employees, this power does not always translate to these problems When managers strive to help someone, they naturally assume the perspective of this person. They accommodate the needs of this individuals, almost involuntarily (Mast, Jonas & Hall 2009).

During job interviews, applicants cannot usually steer the conversation towards drawing uppercase Es on their respective foreheads. They might uncover other cues as to whether the manager or supervisor has considered their perspective.

For example, sometimes the managers will need to write some note on a piece of paper. If these managers write upside down, or rotate the paper, they have most likely considered your perspective. Similarly, on other occasions, the managers might want to show you a letter or article. If these managers rotate the paper or booklet to enable you to read the message, they have also probably considered your perspective. These managers will, most likely, be more helpful than other supervisors.

> ✓ Often, manages will write upside down, or rotate some paper, to enable you to read some note or article. These managers are likely to be understanding and helpful whenever possible.

Part E

The Final Evaluation

Chapter 13

The workgroup

As you wait to be interviewed, you shift your gaze to a bulletin board. On this board is a photograph of 20 or so individuals – individuals with whom you might be working in the future – all smiling genuinely and gleefully. After a few minutes, some of these employees walk past you. One of these individuals has yet to change after riding her bike into work. Another pair of individuals speak to each other. The younger person in this pair speaks very courteously and formally to the older person, calling him Mr Anderson. You become aware of one concern, but decide to inhibit this doubt until after the interview...

Before you accept your job, you could attempt to gather information about your prospective colleagues. You could observe photographs of these individuals on bulletin boards or other forums. If you know their names, you could also unearth some insights about these individuals on facebook or other websites.

If possible, you should even watch these individuals interact with each other and their manager. You might be able to observe these people while waiting to be interviewed – or perhaps while pretending to wait for some other event, such as a friend to arrive. Alternatively, at times the manager may grant you an opportunity to meet everyone before you need to accept the job.

Feigning a genuine smile

Disappointed – the emotion that people usually feel as soon as they see the photo on their driving license. Distraught – the emotion they feel when a friend claims the photo is flattering.

People often complain about the photo on their driving license, passport or company ID card. Most of these people, however, are not aware that, arguably, these photos can actually damage their wellbeing and confidence.

Specifically, some people are genuinely smiling in these photographs. Therefore, almost every day these people observe themselves smiling happily. Over time, they associate themselves with these pleasant features. They begin to perceive themselves favorably. Their sense of confidence, esteem and pride tend to escalate. They become resilient, willing to participate in activities that bolster their skills and extend their experiences.

Research has, to some degree, confirmed this possibility. In one study, some participants repeatedly observed their name followed by a happy face. Other participants repeatedly observed their name followed by an anxious face.

If their name had been continually paired with a happy face, these participants were later more composed, rather than defensive or aggressive, during a subsequent interaction (Baccus, Baldwin & Packer 2004). Somehow, these individuals had learnt to associate a feature of themselves, in this instance their name, with a happy expression. Over time, they became increasingly likely to perceive their features – and hence themselves – favorably. Their self esteem, in essence, increased significantly.

In contrast, some people are not smiling genuinely in these photographs. They may seem grim or inexpressive. Alternatively, their smile might appear contrived or insincere.

These individuals are not as likely to perceive themselves favorably over time. They are not as resilient, but instead are often more defensive and even volatile. Because of their volatility, colleagues need to be wary.

In some organizations, employees are obliged to display their ID card at all times. This card, for example, might be attached to a lanyard or a pocket.

Usually, you can readily ascertain whether their smile on this photograph is genuine, called a Duchenne smile. That is, some smiles do not seem genuine. The mouth might be turned up, but the corners around the eyes are not crinkled. Duchenne smiles in contrast appear to be genuine. The corners around the eyes are wrinkled – a muscular movement that is difficult to control voluntarily.

In other organizations, employees do not display their ID card at all times. However, photographs of the employees might appear in a prominent location, perhaps in the reception area. Even in this instance, employees who observe themselves smiling every day are more likely to become more stable, rather than defensive, over time. Their colleagues do not need to be as wary.

> ✓ Sometimes, the colleagues with whom you might be working need to display their ID cards. Alternatively, photographs of these employees might appear in a prominent location, perhaps in the reception area. If these individuals seem to be smiling genuinely, they are more likely to be stable instead of volatile, and are more likely to feel a sense of control instead of uncertainty.

Two faced book

In addition to ID cards or bulletin boards, information about peers can also be extracted from facebook. Admittedly, facebook is not usually regarded as the most accurate source of information about people. In general, most people do not concede their most debilitating limitations on social networking sites, such as facebook, Twitter, myspace, LinkedIn, Classmates.com, Windows Live Spaces, Tagged, or Bebo. These sites do not usually enable individuals to indicate, for example, whether or not they still wet their bed.

Nevertheless, these sites are, indeed, a key source of important information. To illustrate, some researchers, in 2008, examined whether the profile of individuals on facebook was associated with their personality. Specifically, these researchers assessed many of the characteristics that differentiate these profiles: number of friends, frequency of status updates, and many other features. They also administered a questionnaire intended to gauge the personality of individuals.

Some of these characteristics, such as number of friends, did indeed predict the personality of individuals (Buffardi & Campbell 2008). For example, if the individuals had formed many friends – perhaps over 500 – they were more likely to exhibit the signs of narcissism.

In particular, these individuals were more likely to perceive themselves as special and unique, frequently observing themselves in the mirror. However, .despite this lofty perception of themselves, they were especially brittle. Whenever their opinions are challenged, such people tend to become incensed or distressed. If their behaviour is criticized, they often respond aggressively, with a torrent of furious rejoinders.

Their volatility may contaminate the work environment. Their colleagues, sometimes including their managers, are often vigilant, concerned they might elicit an outburst. The surroundings seem unpredictable.

Some other characteristics of profiles may also signify narcissism. Narcissistic are particularly likely to emphasizes their strengths and achievements. In their profile, they might allude to their qualities or qualifications, such as 'I am an excellent communicator' or 'I am cool under pressure'. In their status updates, they describe each goal they accomplish. They seem to assume that status updates are specifically intended to raise their status.

✓ Sometimes, the colleagues with whom you might be working may exhibit the signs of narcissism in their profile on facebook or other social networking sites. They may have formed more friends or connections that most other people, perhaps 500 or more. They may have enumerated many of their strengths or achievements. These colleagues tend to cultivate an unpredictable and volatile atmosphere.

Slow up

Governments or political parties often disseminate their messages on TV. In many nations, towards the end of these messages or advertisements, the affiliation of this party is revealed.

For example, in Australia, the phrase 'Authorized by the Australian Government Canberra' is often uttered quickly at the end of these commercials. Unfortunately, because the phrase is uttered so hastily, this representative sounds rushed and hurried – as though he is frantic and hysterical, overwhelmed with work and uncertain how to proceed. The government is depicted as hassled and harried, unable to manage the nation.

Indeed, employees often feel rushed and hurried at work. They frequently feel inundated with too many demands and unfeasible targets. Workloads that seem unsustainable are indeed sustained over months or even years.

In one accounting firm, several years ago, an employee attempted to endure a severe migraine at work. After about ten minutes, however, she fainted on the chair. When she regained awareness, she recognized that she needed to leave immediately and telephoned a taxi. As she entered the taxi, one of her managers scurried towards her, opened the door, and heaved her out of the vehicle, shouting 'You still haven't completed the Telstra report!'

The detrimental effects of unrelenting workloads are usually underestimated. Many people, admittedly, know that unyielding stress can provoke burnout and impair their immune system, increasing the likelihood of disease. Fewer people, however, may recognize that taxing workloads, over months or years, can also elicit a host of other problems: regrettable decisions, volatile outbursts, substance abuse, problem gambling, and many other impulsive behaviours.

Specifically, when individuals feel overwhelmed with demands, they are granted few, if any, opportunities to contemplate their future. Their attention is, almost invariably, diverted to pressing obligations instead of future goals. Their thoughts may be oriented towards a shortfall that must be resolved immediately, such as a late report, rather than a grander aspiration, like a business they would like to launch in the future. Their life, often, seems like an inexorable series of isolated tasks, not a meaningful existence with an enduring purpose.

Nevertheless, even when managers do not impose implausible demands, some employees feel hassled. That is, the degree to which employees feel rushed partly depends on the culture and climate of the workplace. As research indicates, when some employees work extensively and intensely, their colleagues are also more likely to feel utterly burdened by relentless demands (Thompson, Beauvais & Lyness 1999). These colleagues, often inadvertently, assume that such intense labor is actually warranted.

In contrast, when some employees do not seem as besieged by hollow demands – but instead grant themselves the time and opportunities to contemplate the future and pursue their aspirations – their colleagues do not feel as hassled. These colleagues also become more sensitive to their own core needs and enduring values. They begin to undertake activities that are more meaningful. Their behaviour becomes more responsible than impulsive. Their stress diminishes, and their volatility subsides.

One Canadian company epitomizes this atmosphere. Every afternoon, at 2.00 pm, employees and managers suspend their work for one hour. They all dedicate this time to any hobby they choose – cooking, sewing or painting, for example – provided they interact with a colleague during this activity.

> ✔ Sometimes, you can derive information about the interests or pursuits of potential colleagues. This information might appear on social networking sites. Alternatively, you might be granted an opportunity to converse with these people before you accept the job. You may discover that some of these individuals experience the time and motivation to contemplate their goals and pursue meaningful activities. For example, a proportion of employees may not be employed full time, but work on personal endeavors on other days. Some employees may cycle to work or undertake various activities that indicate they are not rushed. Other employees may pursue some of their interests at work, such as cook lunch or attend to an indoor garden at work. If this mindset is encouraged, you will feel the goals of this work environment are cohesive. You will not feel bombarded by conflicting expectations.

Disrespectful courtesy

Sometimes you might be granted an opportunity to watch how your potential colleagues interact with their supervisor or manager. You might be able to observe these individuals surreptitiously, perhaps while waiting to be interviewed.

Most people would not want to work at organizations in which employees demonstrate utter disdain towards their managers. They would not want their colleagues, for example, to drop their trousers and display their bottoms whenever their manager imposed a demand.

Nevertheless, the polar opposite of this disdain is disheartening as well. In some organizations, employees tend to be especially polite to managers. They address these individuals with deference. They begin questions with apologies, like 'excuse me' or 'sorry to bother you'. Their language is formal and ceremonial, beginning requests with phrases such as 'would it be acceptable if I' instead of merely 'can I'. They shun colloquialisms.

Such pronounced courtesy and formality tends to indicate a sense of detachment or distance between employees and managers. That is, as investigations have recently shown, when individuals do not feel close to someone, they are more inclined to speak politely (Elana, Liberman & Trope 2010). Furthermore, as they display this courtesy, they begin to feel even more distant from this person.

Therefore, when employees are especially polite to managers, the organization is likely to be very hierarchical. That is, the organization advocates distance and detachment between consecutive levels of management. This hierarchy has been shown to inhibit cooperation and collaboration, as employees and managers become especially motivated to ascend the chain of command.

Furthermore, and somewhat paradoxically, when employees are especially polite because the organization is hierarchical, managers are often disrespectful and unsupportive. That is, in hierarchical organizations, managers tend to convince themselves their position and privileges are warranted. They like to believe they are inherently superior to the employees who are not granted these responsibilities.

As research has substantiated, when managers adopt this belief, their style of leadership is tarnished. They are not as sensitive to the emotions and needs of other people (Nicol 2009). They cannot inspire or accommodate these employees. The organization seems inconsiderate and unsupportive.

> ✗ Sometimes, before you accept a job, you might be

granted the opportunity to observe employees interacting with managers. If these employees demonstrate unmitigated courtesy and deference, by speaking politely and formally, the organization is likely to be very hierarchical. You are unlikely to feel that managers are supportive or that your suggestions will be considered, curbing any sense of control.

The balance of power

In some workgroups, many of the employees are introverted, reserved, and perhaps awkward in social settings. In other workgroups, many of the employees are more extraverted: their demeanor is brash as well as confident, and they speak frequently, without inhibitions or reticence.

In some organizations, introverted applicants are more likely to be selected. That is, relative to their extraverted counterparts, introverted people tend to be more knowledgeable. They are also more vigilant and reliable, and better able to maintain attention during monotonous activities (Rose et al. 2002).

In other organizations, extraverted applicants are more likely to be selected. These individuals are more likely to overestimate their knowledge and skills; they will, therefore, often depict themselves more favorably. Furthermore, extraverted people are sometimes more likely to express original ideas (Furnham & Nederstrom 2010).

Interestingly, subtle features of the surrounding environment, even the weather, influences whether the organization prefers extraverted or introverted people. As some captivating studies have shown, on sunny days managers prefer extraverted people (Simonsohn 2007). Specifically, they are more inclined to recruit individuals with exemplary social skills. On rainy days, managers are not as likely to value these social skills. They are instead more likely to recruit thoughtful, reflective and thus introverted individuals.

To demonstrate, throughout their life, on sunny days people are more likely to attend social gatherings. At these events, individuals like to be confident and sociable. They would often like to be extraverted. Therefore, as the sun appears, individuals are more inclined to value extraversion, and confident, sociable, bold and even dominating employees are preferred.

On rainy days, people are not as likely to attend social gatherings. They are more inclined to contemplate their life and resolve their problems. During these times, they would like to be thoughtful and reflective. As the rain descends, individuals become more inclined to value introversion, and thus reserved and thoughtful employees are preferred.

Therefore, in many organizations a blend of extraverted and introverted people tend to pervade the organization. Nevertheless, in some workgroups almost everyone is either conspicuously introverted or conspicuously extraverted. That is, some teams do not comprise a blend of sociable and reserved – or a combination of dominating and reticent – employees.

If teams do not comprise a blend of extraverted and introverted people, several problems are more prevalent. For example, these teams do not tend to perform as effectively as other workgroups. They are not as efficient or productive (Neuman, Wagner & Christiansen 1999). They are more likely to conflict with one another, rather than work cohesively and seamlessly, and they are more inclined to feel competitive instead of cooperative.

Specifically, when teams comprise a combination of extraverted and introverted people, each individual will naturally and spontaneously gravitate towards a specific role. Some of the most extraverted, dominating individuals will often guide the conversation and reach bold decisions. Some of the most introverted, reflective individuals will often deliberate over matters and identify complications. Over time, everyone feels important; they appreciate their role, even if not prescribed formally. They feel connected to the team, fostering cooperation and collaboration.

If the level of extraversion does not vary across the workgroup, these roles do not materialize as seamlessly. For example, when all the employees are especially extraverted, they might all be attracted to a similar role, such as leading discussions. When all the employees are especially introverted, they might all want to solve problems and consider matters more systematically. These individuals never feel like they have secured a distinct role in the work environment, and they may not feel as appreciated. They will not, therefore, become as committed to the team, impeding cooperation and inducing competition instead.

> * In some workgroups, everyone seems extraverted. In other workgroups, everyone seems introverted. These workgroups are often quite competitive, replete with conflicts. The employees also do not feel they have established a distinct role; they are not as proud of their contributions.

In short, a blend of introverted and extraverted individuals is beneficial. Nevertheless, when some of the individuals are especially introverted or especially extraverted, several problems are more probable. For example, the extent to which individuals are introverted or extraverted changes over time. Some individuals, when young, are especially reserved, shy and awkward. However, if these individuals thrive at work and enjoy their job, they often become more confident and assertive over time, and become more likely to epitomize the qualities of extraverts.

Research has confirmed this possibility. In one study, the personality of over 1,000 participants, aged between 16 and 70, were assessed five times, between the years 1981 and 1989. In addition, the extent to which individuals were satisfied with their work was also measured. If individuals were satisfied at work, they tended to become more extraverted over time. If individuals were dissatisfied, they did not become more extraverted over time and, in some instances, became more introverted (Scollon & Diener 2006).

So, when the work environment is particularly fulfilling, employees will tend to become more confident and sociable over time. When the work environment is unfulfilling and unsatisfying, introverted employees will not become more confident and sociable over time.

The personality of employees, therefore, offers some insight into the climate of this organization. If some of the employees have worked at the organization several years but appear to be especially shy, awkward and reserved, they are unlikely to be satisfied with their job. They are not likely to feel the work is fulfilling or the environment is supportive.

> **✗** In particular workgroups, some of the employees, despite working at the organization over several years, seem especially shy, awkward and reserved. Their demeanor indicates the job might not be especially fulfilling and satisfying.

In addition, people who are very extraverted are often particularly impulsive (Hirsch *et al.* 2010). Their decisions are often rash and their behaviours are often reckless. When angry, they will often launch into a bitter tirade of disparaging remarks. When frustrated, they might reverse a previous decision unexpectedly and abruptly. Other employees, therefore, become wary rather than feel secure.

> **✗** In particular workgroups, some of the individuals are especially uninhibited, bold and extraverted. The other employees often feel wary.

Chapter 14

Rules and prohibitions

As you arrive, minutes before your final interview, you scan the work environment. Many of the work desks are decorated with an assortment of personal adornments like photographs, posters, cartoons or ornaments. After the interview, you receive a job contract and policy document. The policy document includes a series of regulations such as 'No romantic relationships between colleagues are permitted'. Everything seems fine, apart from one doubt...

Employees are often exposed to a barrage of regulations and prohibitions. Signs might appear on walls prohibiting a variety of behaviours, from speaking too loudly to abusing drugs. Policy documents, although not always accessible to job applicants, might include hundreds of additional rules and directives. Other regulations can be extrapolated from a brief observation of the work environment. For example, if all the desks are bare, devoid of photographs or other personal items, you can assume these adornments are prohibited. Although often necessary, and even helpful, some prohibitions elicit a vast sequence of unintended complications.

Decorated desks

In some organizations, employees are granted considerable autonomy. They can prioritize their tasks. They can decide which techniques or procedures to apply to complete their work activities. Their opinions are sought, and their preferences are accommodated.

In other organizations, employees are granted little autonomy. They must adhere to a precise schedule, conform to an established set of procedures, and follow a suite of regulations that encroach on their needs. They would be granted more autonomy if they resigned from the organization and, instead, joined the muppets to become a marionette.

Because their sense of autonomy is impeded, these individuals do not experience a feeling of control over their lives. They do not feel they can prevent unforeseen or unwanted adversities. They feel vulnerable and exposed, often manifesting as anxiety and agitation.

In practice, when candidates seek a job, they are usually assured they will be granted at least some, and usually considerable, autonomy. Managers will seldom boast: 'We get our kicks from treating employees like robots.' Nevertheless, a few telling cues often indicate that employees might be treated like robots rather than people.

For example, in some organizations, employees are not permitted to decorate their desks. Photographs, mementos, souvenirs and other adornments are prohibited. Every desk or workstation must be indistinguishable.

Two significant problems, and negligible benefits, emanate from this policy. First, as research indicates, individuals are not as likely to feel committed, loyal or attached to their workplace. They do not feel proud of their organization (Knight & Haslam 2010).

That is, when employees are granted opportunities to personalize their workspace – e.g. to introduce personal possessions – they develop a sense of connection to the organization, and experience a sense of familiarity.

In contrast, when employees are not permitted to personalize their workspace, they do not develop this sense of connection. They feel alienated and detached. Consequently, they are not as inclined to sacrifice their immediate, personal interests to facilitate the key, future objectives of the organization. They are not as willing to complete tasks they do not enjoy. Employees do not collaborate and coordinate their activities effectively, and the workplace becomes inefficient and unsupportive.

Second, some personal items are especially likely to foster a sense of resilience and to improve wellbeing. Photographs of trusted friends, partners and relatives, for example, have been shown to alleviate stress, anxiety and worry. When individuals are exposed to these photos, they can withstand stressful tasks more effectively. They embrace challenges, such as improvised speeches. These challenges facilitate development and progress.

Similarly, after employees observe one of these photographs, they become more persistent and resilient. To illustrate, in one study, some but not all of the participants were exposed to a photograph of their romantic partner. Next, the participants needed to immerse their hand in very cold water – a task that elicits discomfort and pain. If participants had been exposed to a photograph of their romantic partner, they could more readily withstand this pain (Master et al. 2009). They could submerge their hand in this very cold water over a longer period.

Photographs of family or friends do not enhance only resilience. Interesting, these photographs also promote moral and cooperative, instead of duplicitous or illicit, behaviour as well. That is, when individuals are exposed to supportive people, their motivation to cooperate tends to supersede any motivations to compete.

To clarify, when aware of their friends or relatives, individuals often feel the need to maintain these relationships rather than pursue their personal goals. They will, therefore, strive to fulfill the standards, norms and expectations of these people. That is, they feel compelled to behave morally and cooperatively.

In contrast, if the environment is devoid of friends or relatives, individuals no longer experience this profound need to maintain their relationships. Their compulsion to behave morally wanes. For example, as scientists have shown, after individuals reminisce about a supportive and loving partner, relative or friend, they subsequently become less inclined to cheat on a test (Gillath *et al.* 2010).

Finally, many other studies have also confirmed that pictures of close friends and supportive families foster mutual respect and understanding. For example, when individuals are exposed to photographs or reminders of kind people, they also become more forgiving. If offended or disappointed by someone else, they will not sustain resentment or rage. Even when the name of a close friend or supportive relative is presented subliminally – that is, too rapidly to be recognized consciously – these individuals are more inclined to forgive readily (Karremans & Aarts 2007).

> ✻ In some workplaces, the desks or work stations of employees are devoid of personal items such as photographs, accessories and mementos. Sometimes, official regulations or signs in the office prohibit these items. In these workplaces, colleagues and managers may not seem as supportive. Your autonomy is also restricted. Finally, you do not feel resilient enough to challenge yourself and develop your qualities, compromising your contribution to the workplace.

Impersonal space

In some organizations, employees are not even granted their own desk or workspace at all. That is, many organizations have introduced the concept of hot desking. In these organizations, employees do not work at the same workstation or desk every day. Instead, individuals are allocated the first desk that is available. If they arrive at 8.50 am, they might be assigned a desk in a quiet, secluded area of the building. If they arrive at 8.55 am, however, they might be assigned another desk, perhaps in an area that is not as isolated.

Hot desking is sometimes beneficial. In one European organization, an intelligence agency wanted to monitor an employee, suspected of tax crimes. One evening, these operatives entered the premises and installed a listening device to his desk. The operatives, however, did not realize the organization had recently introduced a policy of hot desking. Over the next three months, they inadvertently monitored the conservations of other employees.

Obviously, hot desking may also conserve space, potentially diminishing the costs of rent. Nevertheless, this approach does elicit a host of problems. Research has revealed that hot desking undermines cooperation (Millward, Haslam & Postmes 2007).

When individuals are assigned their own desk, they are more likely to feel connected to the team or organization. They are more likely to cherish their environment.

Specifically, individuals tend to value anything they feel they own in some sense. They are therefore more inclined to like their own workspace. These positive feelings then extend to their environment. They often like their colleagues, building and role. They will, therefore, remain committed to the organization. They will sacrifice their time and effort to enhance the company, and will thus work collaboratively and productively.

When hot desking is introduced, these benefits vanish. Employees do not feel a sense of ownership over anything in the organization. They are not as inclined to cherish the environment or work as diligently.

> **✷** Some organizations follow a policy in which employees are not assigned a specific desk or workspace. Instead, every day, these individuals are merely allocated the first desk that is available. In these organizations, you are not as likely to feel the environment is collaborative.

Unconnected

At the same time as hot desking has proliferated, curbing the inclination of employees to work diligently, the demands on employees have escalated dramatically. Many employees work more than 50 hours a week, ultimately compromising both mental and physical health (Bond *et al.* 2003).

Nevertheless, the actual workload of individuals does not always correspond to the perceived workload. That is, some individuals work extensively, over 60 hours a week, but do not feel their workload is excessive. Their perceived workload is not particularly elevated. In stark contrast, some individuals are not assigned many tasks at all, but nevertheless feel overwhelmed. Their perceived workload, but not their actual workload, is high.

Even when the actual workload of individuals is modest or reasonable, the perceived workload can be destructive. Regardless of the hours they actually work or the effort they need to dedicate, individuals who feel their workload is excessive are more susceptible to mental or physical illness (Remus *et al.* 2007).

Many subtle events or polices influence the perceived workload of most employees. To illustrate, when individuals hear gossip – such as salacious rumours about the sexual exploits of their conservative managers – they immediately feel they can afford the time to listen and contribute. Other work activities do not seem as pressing or taxing. In contrast, when a photocopy, midway through duplicating articles, fails to operate properly, individuals immediately feel too busy to follow the instructions and correct the problem. They desert the room furtively, return to their office, and continue their urgent tasks.

More importantly, when individuals feel their discretion and choices are respected, their workload often seems manageable. They do not feel as besieged with duties and demands. However, when individuals feel their discretion and choices are discounted, their workload seems excessive. Stress escalates, and progress diminishes (Karasek 1979).

In many organizations, managers introduce policies and practices that, inadvertently, demonstrate contempt rather than respect, and suspicion rather than trust. They might introduce austere, sweeping regulations.

In some organizations, for example, internet use is prohibited at the office unless it is pertinent to a work activity. This regulation not only demonstrates contempt, increasing the likelihood that employees feel overwhelmed rather than immersed in their work, but can even incite unsuitable use of the internet.

Indeed, when individuals are instructed to abstain from some behaviour, they often feel more compelled to initiate this act. If told to refrain from the web, they experience a stronger inclination to utilize the internet, especially if they tend to be obedient (Adriaanse *et al.* 2011).

Furthermore, as many studies demonstrate, when a particular act is prohibited or monitored, individuals assume this activity must be prevalent. They presume, for example, that many people must utilize the internet to fulfil personal needs rather than work objectives; otherwise, the organization would not feel the obligation to prohibit this behaviour (e.g. Greenberg & Barling 1999). They assume this behaviour, if prevalent, must be condoned by most of their colleagues. They will, therefore, feel more compelled, and not reluctant, to enact this behaviour.

In one Australian organization, although personal internet use and computer games were prohibited, one employee played Tetrus every day. One afternoon, the employee did not realize that a stern and authoritarian manager, unfamiliar with the game, was observing his behaviour. The employee, when later asked to explain his behaviour, maintained that he was not playing a game but attempting to decide which patterns should be used to decorate the walls. Consequently, from that day until now, managers still do not know the actual reason that Tetrus shapes populate the walls of all the offices.

> **✗** At some organizations, employees are not permitted

> to use the internet at work for personal reasons. Only internet sites that are pertinent to their work tasks can be visited. In these workplaces, you are more likely to feel stressed and hassled, compromising any sense of control.

I did not have sexual relations...

When men are exposed to photographs of attractive males on the internet, they are more inclined to endorse ideologies that prohibit sex outside marriage. For example, they are more likely to espouse a conservative religion (Li et al. 2010).

Arguably, when these men observe attractive males, they feel unappealing in comparison. They become concerned, sometimes unconsciously, that perhaps they will not be able to attract women. To prevent other males from enticing all the available females, they espouse an ideology that prohibits sex in many circumstances. If this ideology is instituted, these males feel that at least one female will be available and might reciprocate their advances.

Senior managers might, occasionally, adopt the same rationale. If these managers are unattractive, they might attempt to prohibit sex in some circumstances. They might, for instance, introduce a regulation that forbids romantic liaisons in the workplace.

Admittedly, in many instances, other motives prompt these prohibitions of relationships at work. Regardless of the motives, these regulations are not only common but often destructive.

Just like a rule that prohibits chocolate would not prevent cravings, a rule that prohibits relationships does not prevent attraction. In these environments, if employees feel attracted to one another, two responses are possible. First, they can strive to suppress these feelings. They can attempt to divert their attention elsewhere rather than yield to this desire.

Unfortunately, these feelings, when suppressed, tend to intensify over time. As some experts argue, to suppress these urges, individuals shift their attention to various features in the environment. They might orient their focus to the photocopy machine, to the ceiling fan, to the building outside, to the carpet, and so forth. Over time, however, these individuals then associate each of these items with the object of their desire. The photocopy machine, the ceiling fan, the building outside and the carpet all evoke thoughts and memories of this person (Muris, Merckelbach & Horselenberg 1996). A mild attraction sometimes escalates into a destructive fixation.

Persistent attempts to neglect these powerful urges are more challenging and, ultimately, more exhausting. That is, these attempts consume glucose. Energy reserves in the brain thus dissipate (Gailliot *et al.* 2007). As these reserves subside, any feelings of engagement and dedication evolve into burnout and lethargy. Excitement often translates into irritability. Progress stalls and wellbeing declines.

Alternatively, rather than suppress these urges, individuals may conceal their relationships at work. This arrangement may be adequate at first, but problems may gradually materialize.

Specifically, to maintain the secret, these individuals need to monitor themselves vigilantly and continuously. They cannot refer to their partner inadvertently. Instead, they often need to fabricate details. If they watch a movie with their partner, they might need to concoct another friend when they describe this film to someone else at work. If they are asked whether or not they would consent to a blind date, they might need to contrive a reason to decline.

These individuals, therefore, cannot express their genuine feelings and thoughts. They must incessantly inhibit their cognitions and intuitions. Over time, they even become detached or divorced from their genuine or natural inclinations. Because they cannot as readily access or utilize these natural inclinations, these individuals are often plagued with doubt, uncertainty and hesitation, sometimes culminating in feelings of alienation and futility (Lehmiller 2009).

This secrecy does not only compromise the wellbeing of each person but also tends to impair their relationships. When relationships are public rather than concealed, the two individuals tend to feel their identities overlap. They conceptualize themselves as one union rather than merely two detached people.

To some extent, they feel the qualities and attributes of the other person become part of their own repertoire. If their partner is bold and confident, they also, in some sense, feel they have acquired these traits. If their partner is enlightened about some topic, they also feel they have, in essence, acquired this knowledge. To maintain these qualities, they feel especially motivated to sustain this union. They feel committed to this relationship (Lehmiller 2009).

Once committed, individuals tend to overrate the attributes of their partner. Minor faults are perceived as endearing. Favorable attributes, such as intelligence, are exaggerated. Even conflicts are perceived as fleeting instead of permanent.

In contrast, when relationships are concealed, these benefits are not as common. In these contexts, the individuals cannot refer to one another as 'we' or 'us'. They do not feel their identities overlap but often conceptualize themselves as entirely independent. They do not feel they have acquired the qualities and attributes of the other person. They are not as likely, therefore, to feel committed to the union.

Without this commitment, problems are not overlooked. Conflicts are not assumed to be transient. Consequently, both parties often overreact to minor complications. The relationships, rather than a source of security, may instead provoke anxiety, stress and uncertainty. The mood of these individuals, both at work and at home, thus declines.

Research has confirmed these arguments. As one study showed, relative to their colleagues, employees who conceal their relationships are more likely to experience obvious signs of acute stress. They are more likely to be afflicted with headaches, nausea, digestion problems, fatigue, irritation, loneliness or shakiness (Lehmiller 2009).

✖ Some organizations prohibit romantic relationships between colleagues. In these organizations, you are more likely to feel that colleagues – especially colleagues who are affected by this policy – are unsupportive and volatile.

Chapter 15

Experiments to assess the organization

You decide to observe the employees of this organization as they interact and negotiate with challenging customers. The employees seem very helpful. When the customer drops a purse, the employees immediately retrieve the item. When the customer asks a challenging request, the employees diligently seek a solution. The employees work tirelessly to assist these customers. Indeed, as soon as the customer leaves, the smile that had covered the face of these employees rapidly evolves into a doleful, exhausted expression, until the next customer arrives. The dedication of these employees impresses you. Yet, one problem does seem troubling …

Sometimes, to scrutinize the organization more systematically, you can conduct a series of experiments. You can, for example, test how employees might respond to particular challenges. You can assess how managers answer specific questions, strategically asked to distil important information.

The misdirected email

One technique, sometimes used to discriminate supportive environments from their ruthless counterparts, is called the lost or misdirected email. Your task is to send a few emails to the organization – emails that were supposedly intended to be directed to someone else. An example might be:

Subject: Hospital

Tara

How is everything going? I felt really bad for you last night

When do you want me to pick you up so we can drive to the hospital?

Best wishes

Pete

Hey Pete

About the same. I suppose it's just one of those things

I have time in about an hour to go, so please email me back as soon as you can.

T.

In this instance, Tara needs Pete to drive her to the hospital for an important reason She has, supposedly, misdirected the email to an employee of this organization.

One study showed that, on average, only about 20 percent of people returned this email to the sender, Tara. Almost nobody forwarded the email to the intended receiver, Pete (Stern & Faber 1997).

Interestingly, emails that allude to complex emotions, like hope, enchantment, admiration, disappointment or embarrassment – emotions that only humans rather than animals are likely to experience – are more frequently returned. Emails that do not allude to any emotions at all, or to emotions that animals seem to experience as well, like surprise, anger, fear and lethargy, are seldom returned. As this finding reveals, when individuals do not direct their attention to the humanity of this person, they are not as inclined to return the emails (Vaes, Paladino & Leyens 2002). They feel no compassion or responsibility.

Therefore, in the most competitive environments, these emails will tend to be discarded. Specifically, in these settings, managers often perceive other individuals as instruments to fulfil some other purpose. These individuals are not regarded or treated as sentient human beings but as dehumanized entities. When managers objectify people in this way, they generally do not return the emails. However, in the most cooperative environments, the managers will tend to return the email and offer help.

So, if possible, access an email account that cannot be traced to you. Perhaps establish a gmail account with another name – preferably not the same name you use for facebook or other websites. Alternatively, ask friends whether you could use their account.

Now, if possible, send an email to several people in the organization – ideally managers and supervisors from different teams or departments. Type an email that demands a response. And, then wait for a reply …

> ✓ After sending an email that demands a response sporadically throughout an organization, sometimes over a third or so of these messages are returned. In these organizations, managers tend to show compassion and consideration; the environment is more likely to be cooperative.

An awkward customer

Rather than send misdirected emails, you could also profess to be customer. You could then assess the behaviour of employees to challenging customers – behaviours that offer some insight into the culture and climate of the organization, particularly the fairness of procedures.

That is, in some organizations the rewards, evaluations and procedures are fair and just. Whenever employees need to work late into the evening, striving to fulfill an ambitious deadline, they are compensated appropriately in these organizations. Whenever the performances of employees are appraised, all of their contributions and challenges are considered, without bias or distortion. Whenever problems develop, employees are granted opportunities to voice their concerns. Whenever employees work effectively, their efforts are recognized.

When the organization is fair and just, problems are not as likely to unfold unexpectedly. Employees who work diligently and arduously will not be castigated or criticized unpredictably. Employees who strive to enhance their organization will not be demoted or dismissed abruptly. The environment seems predictable and stable. Employees feel protected enough to extend their skills and to explore their purpose in life, translating to a sense of meaning and wellbeing.

Unfortunately, most job applicants cannot ascertain whether the organization is fair and just. They certainly cannot distil this information from the managers. Even when the organization is plagued with injustice, the managers will tend to be oblivious to these concerns. They will often assume the decisions of their organization are fair. The probability that managers will recognize and concede the organization is unfair is equal to the probability that mothers will recognize and concede their newborn baby is just plain ugly.

Fortunately, applicants can utilize other sources of information to establish whether the organization is unjust. To some extent, they can distill this information from the satisfaction of customers.

When the workplace is unjust, employees do not feel respected. Because they feel unappreciated, these employees, in one sense, do not feel they belong. They feel disconnected or disengaged from the organization rather than committed and loyal. They do not, therefore, feel motivated to enhance the organization. They withdraw effort and dedication.

As an example of injustice, one multinational consulting firm established a practice that is obviously unfair. The practice emanates from a simple argument: if the credibility of a manager is undermined, clients might not trust the firm. If the credibility of a junior employee, however, is undermined, the client might continue to trust the firm. Therefore, whenever the organization commits a serious error, incensing or infuriating a client, at least one novice employee is usually dismissed. Novice employees are blamed, regardless of who had committed or provoked the error.

Indeed, as research indicates, when employees feel the workplace is unjust, customers of this organization tend to be dissatisfied with the services (Masterson 2001). That is, because the employees withhold their effort, they do not strive vigorously to accommodate the needs of their customers. They do not resolve the problems and concerns of these customers promptly or effectively, leaving customers feeling dissatisfied and frustrated.

In contrast, when the workplace is fair, employees are more likely to feel respected and appreciated. They experience a sense of belonging to the organization, escalating their motivation to improve the workplace. They are more inclined to mobilize their effort and to fulfill the needs of their customers.

Therefore, if possible, you should assess the satisfaction of customers or the dedication of employees. For example, in many instances the organization offers services to the general public, such as banking, utilities and clothing. You could ask your friends to evaluate the services of these organizations. Are the employees helpful? Do these employees demonstrate effort and dedication, resolving the problems of customers rapidly and industriously? Are the employees accommodating and flexible in response to challenging requests?

In other instances, you might not know anyone who utilizes the services of this organization. You could, instead, gauge the satisfaction of customers from other sources. For example, you could contact the peak body of this industry – a professional association or registration board perhaps. You could seek information from this body, such as data from a survey, or informal advice about the services of this organization. That is, you could ask: 'Do you have any information about whether customers are satisfied or dissatisfied with the services of this organization?'

Alternatively, you might be able to derive this information from other resources. Some magazines, like Choice, could provide useful data. Internet sites, in which customers express their satisfaction or dissatisfaction, could be informative as well.

If you are still unable to access the requisite data, you could approach employees yourself. You could pretend to seek the services of this organization, posing a challenging request. If the organization sells insurance, you could seek cover for an unusual product or situation. If the company provides catering, you could request a rare dish, and so forth.

✓ Whenever the employees of some organizations interact with a customer, they demonstrate effort and flexibility in their attempts to resolve problems and to help this person. These employees are likely to feel committed and loyal to their organization. This loyalty implies the organization might be just and fair, cultivating a sense of control in employees.

A smile a minute

Laughing schools have become rampant across many nations. During these classes, participants learn how to laugh with gusto, passion and vigor, putatively to improve their health and wellbeing. Indeed, many individuals – perhaps with the exception of people with unreliable bladders – have attended these schools.

Similarly, some organizations have introduced programs in which employees learn how to smile, genuinely and warmly. They learn, for instance, some recent scientific discoveries, such as the finding that smiles that appear gradually, over the course of half a second, are perceived as more genuine than smiles that appear more abruptly (Krumhuber, Manstead & Kappas 2006).

Although these illustrations might seem unusual, programs in which employees learn how to express positive emotions are almost ubiquitous. Many employees are instructed to conceal negative emotions: anger, frustration, stress, worry, lethargy and disgust, for example. These individuals are encouraged to demonstrate a sanguine demeanor, regardless of the circumstances. Whenever they interact with customers, they need to seem excited, optimistic, supportive or content.

Over the last decade, many studies have revealed that such practices can be damaging. When individuals need to seem positive, despite their frustration, stress or other unpleasant states, they must suppress or contain their actual feelings. They need to monitor themselves vigilantly and exhaustively. Because of these demands, they are more likely to feel exhausted after work. They often experience a sense of futility and isolation rather than meaning and purpose (Brotheridge & Grandey 2002).

In one café, just outside New York, the owner attached a sign, near the counter, reading 'Chicken sandwiches are not available today'. Despite this sign, a customer demanded a chicken sandwich. The owner explained, calmly and patiently, this item was not available today because the ingredients had already been consumed. Two minutes later, another customer also ordered a chicken sandwich. Again, the owner had to explain the sandwiches were unavailable. Every two minutes, another customer would order the same dish. Every two minutes, the owner would explain, with escalating composure and patience, that chicken sandwiches were not available. Eventually, after the twentieth or so customer ordered the same dish, the owner exploded, yelling 'Oh for god sake, you idiot. Can't you read. What the hell is wrong with you'.

Furthermore, after employees are instructed to monitor and suppress their actual emotions, they are more likely to be evaluated negatively by customers. Customers feel the emotions of these employees are feigned. At some level, they recognize the facial expressions and mannerisms of these employees are not consistent with each other. These incongruities evoke a sense of uncertainty in customers – a feeling that compromises their satisfaction (Grandey 2003).

Observations of employees who interact with customers, therefore, can be very informative. Sometimes, after they end a conversation with a customer, their facial expression changes abruptly. A smile is supplanted instantly with a frown, scowl, or some other unpleasant expression. These abrupt shifts usually imply the original smile was feigned. In these organizations, the employees have probably been instructed to exhibit a particular demeanor. The emotions of employees are regulated and monitored closely. They often feel exhaustion but act as if they are happy.

> ✘ If the organization offers services to the general public, you should observe the employees who interact with customers. Sometimes, after the employees complete a transaction with a customer, their smile almost immediately evolves into an unpleasant expression. In these organizations, employees are likely to experience burnout. The environment is seldom collaborative.

The calculated clutz

Some experiments should be directed towards the people with whom you might be working: your manager or peers, for example. These experiments are intended to ascertain whether these people are cooperative. Some experiments, for example, can be readily conducted during a job interview.

Although not always applicable to job applicants, scientists have develop many ruses to establish whether or not someone is helpful, supportive and cooperative. They might, for example, present willing participants a series of words. However, some of the letters are replaced by dashes, like co - pe - - tive. The participants are then instructed to identify the words.

Many people assume this task is merely intended to measure their verbal skills or abilities. However, unbeknownst to participants, this task actually assesses whether people are helpful and supportive or unhelpful and competitive.

To illustrate, the answer to co - pe - - tive could be cooperative or competitive. People who assume the answer is cooperative tend to be more helpful and supportive in general. They perceive individuals as trustworthy and dependable. People who assume the answer is competitive may not be as helpful and supportive (Bartz & Lydon 2004).

During job interviews, however, managers do not like to complete word puzzles. Nevertheless, if you are adventurous, you might consider another ruse, occasionally utilized and validated by scientists (e.g. Warneken & Tomasello 2008) to assess whether the managers are supportive.

Towards the end of this interview, as you prepare to leave, you could surreptitiously drop an item – perhaps a pen or sheet of paper – to the floor. After you release the item, wait a few seconds as you pretend to organize your other possessions.

This technique offers you an opportunity to gauge the behaviour of this person. Cooperative managers will tend to retrieve the item or at least offer some assistance. Competitive managers will never almost never offer this assistance.

> ✓ Sometimes, after you drop an item, either deliberately or accidentally, during an interview, the manager will offer some assistance. These managers tend to be cooperative in general, cultivating a more supportive environment.

The calculated questions

Finally, strategic questions, perhaps during the job interviews with managers, can also uncover some key information about the organization. In response to these questions, managers will sometimes, often unwittingly, articulate a response that reveals the workplace environment is probably unsupportive and disrespectful.

This information can be derived from idle gossip. Most people like to gossip. People who often say 'I don't like to gossip, but...' especially like to gossip. In particular, to feel superior, people especially like to gossip about flaws – about people who behaved immorally, inanely or inappropriately.

This inclination can be exploited in job interviews. Managers will seldom concede that members of their own workgroup are aggressive, offensive or disrespectful. They are, however, often willing to admit that individuals in other workgroups or departments behave inappropriately. They might, for example, insist that 'those guys in the accounts department are sometimes just plain rude'. Alternatively, they might imply, perhaps more subtly, that other workgroups or departments might sometimes behave offensively, with observations like 'Some of other teams are not as civil as our workgroup'.

At first glance, you might assume that offensive behaviour, confined to other workgroups, might not be too concerning, especially if you do not often interact with these individuals. You might feel that only the behaviour and decorum of your own team, workgroup or department is integral to your experience at work. However, as recent investigations have persuasively revealed, the offensive behaviour of one workgroup can undermine the culture, cohesion and capabilities of other workgroups as well, at least in particular circumstances.

That is, when individuals merely observe offensive behaviour, their own conduct often changes significantly. After these observations, people feel, often unconsciously, that the environment is not cohesive. They feel the surroundings are divided and threatening, at least to some extent. Consequently, they experience an impulse to be competitive instead of cooperative. They become more inclined to act unsupportively, even duplicitously, to fulfill their personal needs.

In one study, for example, participants observed rude behaviour between two strangers from afar. After they observed this offensive interaction, the participants were not as inclined to help someone else (Porath & Erez 2009). Indeed, because they felt the environment was not cohesive, their concentration deteriorated. Their performance on a subsequent creative task, for example, declined.

Thus, during job interviews, you should attempt to gauge the behaviour of other workgroups in the same vicinity or floor – workgroups that you are likely to observe. You could ask, somewhat casually: 'Which departments do we interact with most frequently' or 'What are some of the other departments on this floor'.

Then, when the managers answer, you could ask: 'How do they feel about our work?' or some other question intended to steer the conversation to the behaviour of these teams or departments. If the manager concedes the behaviour of these teams or department is sometimes disrespectful, you might consider the possibility that members of your own workgroup might be competitive or aggressive as well.

> ✘ Sometimes, the manager concedes that some of the other teams or departments that you are likely to observe are often disrespectful or even offensive. This disrespect often increases the likelihood that your own team might be competitive instead of cooperative.

Chapter 16

Concluding comments

Resilience without reality

The contents of this book, although validated by scientific research, nevertheless can evoke some controversies. Some practitioners, for example, maintain that organizations do not need to introduce blue walls, curved furniture, naked light bulbs, personalized desks, a youthful brand, effeminate or female directors, or any of the other practices recommended in this volume to inspire employees. Instead, they assume that many of the existing initiatives are sufficient.

Indeed, many organizations introduce programs, including workshops and other provisions, that are intended to enhance the resilience of employees. A series of insights are imparted, and exercises are encouraged, all intended to curb anxiety and apprehension in unpredictable and challenging environments. Individuals might, for example, learn how to withstand setbacks, embrace challenges, think optimistically, pursue aspirations, and develop confidence.

Unfortunately, initiatives that purportedly enhance resilience are often ineffective and even destructive. To illustrate, a multitude of events, beginning in childhood and continuing to adulthood, affect the resilience of individuals. In addition, many biological attributes also shape resilience. Therefore, to cultivate resilience, individuals would actually need to undertake a diversity of exercises. They may need to write constructively about previous traumas. They may need to learn how to direct their attention to supportive people (Dandeneau *et al.* 2007). Indeed, they may need to complete many activities spanning months, and sometimes years.

However, organizations cannot afford to cultivate resilience over years. Instead, they seek brief alternatives – programs that can be completed within a day or two. Organizations often, therefore, engage the services of consultants who promulgate simple mottos like 'Think positively', 'Maintain your optimism', or 'Emphasize your strengths'.

These mottos cannot override the origins of anxiety or instability. The sources of these emotions persist.

Indeed, these mottos elicit thoughts that contradict the natural inclinations of individuals. Individuals are invited to think positively, even if at some level they experience grave doubts. They are implored to be optimistic, despite a cynicism that evolved over many years.

Consequently, individuals experience a sense of conflict. After they complete these programs, the employees feel compelled to confine their thoughts to positive and desirable opportunities and possibilities. Nevertheless, because of their experiences, they feel a profound inclination to consider the problems, complications, drawbacks and obstacles that might unfold. They experience conflicting desires – a contradiction that tends to stifle their motivation and provoke burnout.

Furthermore, as individuals strive vigorously to override their cynical thoughts and negative emotions, their warmth and compassion declines. Admittedly, when these people are informed that one or two people have been killed in an accident, they exhibit some compassion. However, when informed that hundreds, if not thousands, of people have been killed in a natural disaster, they seem aloof and uncaring.

This possibility has been substantiated by scientists (Cameron & Payne 2011). Specifically, if employees attempt to override negative thoughts or unpleasant feelings, natural disasters and other misfortunes do not evoke compassion. They recognize, perhaps unconsciously, that compassion towards thousands of people could elicit a torrent of unpleasant emotions. Therefore, to enhance their immediate emotions, they withdraw this compassion and seem detached and unfeeling.

Competitive benefits of cooperative behaviour

This decline in warmth and compassion, however, does not disturb some managers. That is, some managers contend that business revolves around money and not meaning, around competition and not cooperation.

However, these managers neglect some key considerations. Specifically, cooperation improves performance, fundamentally and sustainably. Hundreds of reasons underpin this association between cooperation and performance, between a supportive environment and a thriving workplace.

To illustrate one reason, when people feel their colleagues are supportive, loyal and understanding, they are more confident they can surmount any obstacles that transpire. That is, after individuals interact with a supportive person – a close friend, a cherished relative or a trusted colleague, for example – taxing activities immediately seem feasible.

In one study, participants were told they must traverse a steep hill. Before they attempted this task, some of the participants were granted an opportunity to interact with a supportive person. Compared to other participants, these individuals felt the hill did not seem unbearably steep (Schnall *et al.* 2008). They felt confident they could accomplish this objective – a sense of confidence that translates into persistence and ultimately success. A competitive orientation, in contrast, tends to impair confidence, learning, creativity and resilience (Dweck 2006).

Success should not emanate from the inexorable motivation to outperform competitors. Instead, only the passion to pursue a purpose – and the determination to impart a distinct contribution – should inspire the progress and performance of individuals and organizations.

Work and life

A competitive orientation may not only impair performance but incites problems that infiltrate every facet of our being. In competitive environments, everyone wants to be perceived as proficient. They want to accentuate their merits and conceal their imperfections. They seldom concede their limitations, anxieties or concerns.

When these anxieties and concerns are concealed, rather than disclosed, employees tend to underestimate the frequency of these problems. They assume, often incorrectly, that most of their colleagues are content and excited. They presume these people are, almost invariably, unfettered by feelings of apprehension, dejection, shame, or other unpleasant states.

Therefore, whenever employees in these organizations are anxious or upset, not only do they conceal these emotions but they also feel isolated and alienated as well. They feel ashamed that only they are experiencing this pain or distress. Research has indeed confirmed that such work environments – environments in which people mask their emotions – represent one of the main causes of rampant loneliness and depression (Jordan *et al.* 2011). Modern organizations represent the font of many problems and thus a source of many opportunities.

References

Aaker, J. , Fournier, S., & Brasel, S. A. (2004). When good brands do bad. *Journal of Consumer Research*, 31, 1-16.

Aarts, H., & Dijkersterhuis, A. (2003). The silence of the library: Environment, situational norms, and social behavior. *Journal of Personality and Social Psychology*, 84, 18-28.

Adriaanse, M. A., de Ridder, D. T. D., & de Wit, J. B. F. (2009). Finding the critical cue: Implementation intentions to change one's diet work best when tailored to personally relevant reasons for unhealthy eating. *Personality and Social Psychology Bulletin*, 35, 60-71.

Adriaanse, M. A., van Oosten, J. M. F., de Ridder, D. T. D., de Wit, J. B. F., & Evers, C. (2011). Planning what not to eat: Ironic effects of implementation intentions negating unhealthy habits. *Personality and Social Psychology Bulletin*, 37, 69-81.

Akehurst, L., Bull, R., Vrij, A., & Köhnken, G. (2004). The effects of training professional groups and lay persons to use Criteria-Based Content Analysis to detect deception. *Applied Cognitive Psychology*, 18, 877-891.

Anolli, L., & Ciceri, R. (1997). The voice of deception: Vocal strategies of naïve and able liars. *Journal of Nonverbal Behavior*, 21, 259-284.

Arnulf, J. K., Tegner, L., & Larssen, O. (2010). Impression making by resume layout: Its impact on the probability of being shortlisted. *European Journal of Work and Organizational Psychology*, 19, 221-230.

Avramova, Y. R., & Stapel, D. A. (2008). Mood as spotlights: The influence of mood on accessibility effects. *Personality and Individual Differences*, 95, 542

Baccus, J. R., Baldwin, M. W., & Packer, D. J. (2004). Increasing implicit self-esteem through classical conditioning. *Psychological Science*, 15, 498-502.

Bartz, J. A., & Lydon, J. E. (2004). Close relationships and the working self-concept: Implicit and explicit effects of priming attachment on agency and communion. *Personality and Social Psychology Bulletin*, 30, 1389-1401.

Batson, C. D., Lishner, D. A., Carpenter, A., Dulin, L., Harjusola-Webb, S., Stocks, E. L., et al. (2010). ' . . . as you would have them do unto you': Does imagining yourself in the other's place stimulate moral action? *Personality and Social Psychology Bulletin*, 29, 1190-1201.

Baumann, N., & Kuhl, J. (2003). Self-infiltration: Confusing assigned tasks as self-selected in memory. *Personality and Social Psychology Bulletin*, 29, 487-497.

Baumeister, R. F. (1991). *Meanings of life*. New York: Guilford.

Beeman, M. J., & Bowden, E. M. (2000). The right hemisphere maintains solution-related activation for yet-to-be-solved problems. *Memory & Cognition*, 28, 1231-1241.

Bell, J. D. & Fay, M. T. (1997). A longitudinal study of the attitudes of the medical profession towards competition and advertising. *International Journal of Advertising*, 17, 349-336.

Bond, J., Thompson, C., Galinsky, E., & Prottas, D. (2003). Highlights of the National Study of the Changing Workforce. *Family and Work Institute*, No. 3.

Borton, J. L. S., Markovitz, L. J., & Dieterich, J. (2005). Effects of suppressing negative self-referent thoughts on mood and self-esteem. *Journal of Social and Clinical Psychology*, 24, 172-180.

Brendl, C. M., Chattopadhyay, A., Pelham, B. W., & Carvallo, M. (2005). Name letter branding: Valence transfers when product specific needs are active. *Journal of Consumer Research*, 32, 405-415.

Brennan, A., Chugh, J. S., & Kline, T. (2002). Traditional versus open office design: A longitudinal field study. *Environment and Behavior*, 34, 279-299.

Britt, T. W., Adler, A. B., & Bartone, P. T. (2001). Deriving benefits from stressful events: The role of engagement in meaningful work and hardiness. *Journal of Occupational Health Psychology*, 6, 53-63.

Brotheridge, C. M., & Grandey, A. A. (2002). Emotional labor and burnout: Comparing two perspectives of 'people work'. *Journal of Vocational Behavior*, 60, 17-39.

Buckley, M. R., Mobbs, T. A., Mendoza, J. L., Novicevic, M. M., Carraher, S. M., & Beu, D. S. (2002). Implementing realistic job previews and expectation-lowering procedures: A field experiment. *Journal of Vocational Behavior*, 61, 263-278.

Buffardi, L. E., & Campbell, W. K. (2008). Narcissism and social networking web sites. *Personality and Social Psychology Bulletin*, 34, 1303-1314.

Burson, K. A., Larrick, R. P., & Lynch, Jr. J. G. (2009). Six of one, half dozen of the other: Expanding and contracting numerical dimensions produces preference reversals. *Psychological Science*, 20, 1074-1078.

Butler, J. K. (1999). Trust, expectations, information sharing, climate of trust, and negotiation effectiveness and efficiency. *Group & Organization Management*, 24, 217-238.

Cameron, C. D., & Payne, B. K. (2011). Escaping affect: How motivated emotion regulation creates insensitivity to mass suffering. *Journal of Personality and Social Psychology*, 100, 1-15.

Cascio, W. F. (2002). *Responsible restructuring: Creative and profitable alternatives to layoffs*. San Francisco, Berrett-Koehler.

Caso, L., Maricchiolo, F., Bonaiuto, M., Vrij, A., & Mann, S. (2006). The impact of deception and suspicion on different hand movements. *Journal of Nonverbal Behavior*, 30, 1-19.

Cesario, J., Plaks, J. E., & Higgins, E. T. (2006). Automatic social behavior as motivated preparation to interact. *Journal of Personality and Social Psychology*, 90, 893-910.

Dambrun, M., Kamiejski, R., Haddadi, N., & Duarte, S. (2009). Why does social dominance decrease with university exposure to the social sciences? The impact of institutional socialization and the mediating role of ' geneticism'. *European Journal of Social Psychology*, 39, 88-100.

Dandeneau, S. D., Baldwin, M. W., Baccus, J. R., Sakellaropoulo, M., & Pruessner, J. C. (2007). Cutting stress off at the pass: Reducing vigilance and responsiveness to social threat by manipulating attention. *Journal of Personality and Social Psychology*, 93, 651-666.

Debats, D. L. (1996). Meaning in life: Clinical relevance and predictive power. *British Journal of Clinical Psychology*, 35, 503-516.

Denzler, M., Forster, J., & Liberman, N. (2009). How goal-fulfillment decreases aggression. *Journal of Experimental Social Psychology*, 45, 90-100.

Dijksterhuis, A., Bos, M. W., Nordgren, L. F., & Van Baaren, R. B. (2006). On making the right choice: The deliberation-without-attention effect. *Science*, 311, 1005-1007

Dijksterhuis, A., Bos, M. W., van der Leij, A. & van Baaren, R. B. (2009). Predicting soccer matches after unconscious and conscious thought as a function of expertise. *Psychological Science*, 20, 1381-1387.

Dijksterhuis, A., & van Olden, Z. (2006). On the benefits of thinking unconsciously: Unconscious thought can increase post-choice satisfaction. *Journal of Experimental Social Psychology*, 42, 627-631.

Dweck, C. S. (2006). *Mindset: The new psychology of success*. New York: Random House.

Eidelman, S., Crandall, C. S., & Pattershall, J. (2009). The existence bias. *Journal of Personality and Social Psychology*, 97, 765-775.

Elana, S., Liberman, N., & Trope, Y. (2010). Politeness and psychological distance: A construal level perspective. *Journal of Personality and Social Psychology*, 98, 268-280.

Ellis, L., Das, S., & Buker, H. (2008). Androgen-promoted physiological traits and criminality: A test of the evolutionary neuroandrogenic theory. *Personality and Individual Differences*, 44,699-709.

Faddegon, K., Scheepers, D., & Ellemers, N. (2008). If we have the will, there will be a way: Regulatory focus as a group identity. *European Journal of Social Psychology*, 38, 880-895.

Fast, N. J., & Chen, S. (2009). When the boss feels inadequate: Power, incompetence, and aggression. *Psychological Science*, 20, 1406-1413.

Fink,B., Hamdaoui, A., Wenig, F., & Neave, N. (2010). Hand-grip strength and sensation seeking. *Personality and Individual Differences*, 49, 789-793.

Fisher, H. E., Rich, J., Island, H. D., & Marchalik, D. (2010). The second to fourth digit ratio: A measure of two hormonally-based temperament dimensions. *Personality and Individual Differences*, 49, 773-777.

Fitzsimons, G. M., Chartrand, T. L., & Fitzsimons, G. J. (2008). Automatic effects of brand exposure on motivated behavior: How apples makes you think different. *Journal of Consumer Research*, 35, 21-35.

Fitzsimons, G. M, & Shah, J. Y. (2008). How goal instrumentality shapes relationship evaluations. *Journal of Personality and Social Psychology*, 95, 319-337.

Fong, C. T. (2006). The effects of emotional ambivalence on creativity. *Academy of Management Journal*, 49, 1016-1030.

Forster, J., & Higgins, E. T. (2005). How global versus local perception fits regulatory focus. *Psychological Science*, 16, 631-636.

Freitas, A. L., Clark, S. L., Kim, J. Y., & Levy, S. R. (2009). Action-construal levels and perceived conflict among ongoing goals: Implications for positive affect. *Journal of Research in Personality*, 43, 938-941.

Friedman, R. S., & Forster, J. (2001). The effects of promotion and prevention cues on creativity. *Journal of Personality and Social Psychology*, 81, 1001-1013.

Furnham, A., & Nederstrom, M. (2010). Ability, demographic and personality predictors of creativity. *Personality and Individual Differences*, 48, 957-961.

Furnham, A., & Walker, J. (2001). Personality and judgements of abstract, pop art, and representational paintings. *European Journal of Personality*, 15, 57-72.

Gailliot, M. T., Baumeister, R. F., DeWall, C. N., Maner, J. K., Plant, E. A., Tice, D. M., et al. (2007). Self-control relies on glucose as a limited energy source: Willpower is more than a metaphor. *Journal of Personality and Social Psychology*, 92, 325-336.

Galinsky, A. D., Magee, J. C., Inesi, M. E., & Gruenfeld, D. H. (2006). Power and perspectives not taken. *Psychological Science*, 17, 1068-1074.

Gillath, O, Secko, A. K. Shaver, P. R., & Chun, D. S. (2010). Attachment, authenticity, and honesty: Dispositional and experimentally induced security can reduce self- and other-deception. *Journal of Personality and Social Psychology*, 98, 841-855.

Gino, F., & Pierce, L. (2009). The abundance effect: Unethical behavior in the presence of wealth. *Organizational Behavior and Human Decision Processes*, 109, 142-155.

Gorn, G. J., Chattopadhyay, A., Sebgupta, J., & Tripathi, S. (2004). Waiting for the web: How screen color affects time perception. *Journal of Marketing Research*, 41, 215-225.

Grandey, A. A. (2003). When 'The show must go on': Surface acting and deep acting as determinants of emotional exhaustion and peer-rated service delivery. *Academy of Management Journal*, 46, 86-96.

Grant, A. M., & Sonnetag, S. (2010). Doing good buffers against feeling bad: Prosocial impact compensates for negative task self-evaluations. *Organizational Behavior and Human Decision Processes*, 111, 13-22.

Greenberg, L., & Barling, J. (1999). Predicting employee aggression against coworkers, subordinates, and supervisors: The roles of person behaviours and perceived workplace factors. *Journal of Organizational Behavior*, 20, 897-913.

Griskevicius, V., Shiota, M. N., & Nowlis, S. M. (2010). The many shades of rose-colored glasses: An evolutionary approach to the influence of different positive emotions. *Journal of Consumer Research*, 37, 238-250.

Griskevicius, V., Tybur, J. M., & Van den Bergh, B. (2010). Going green to be seen: Status, reputation, and conspicuous conservation. *Journal of Personality and Social Psychology*, 98, 392-404.

Heimbeck, D., Frese, M., Sonnentag, S., & Keith, N. (2003). Integrating errors into the training process: The function of error management instructions and the role of goal orientation. *Personnel Psychology*, 56, 333-361.

Heine, S. J., Proulx, T., & Vohs, K. D. (2006). Meaning maintenance model: On the coherence of human motivations. *Personality and Social Psychology Review*, 10, 88-110.

Henkel, L. A. & Mather, M. (2007). Memory attributions for choices: How beliefs shape our memories. *Journal of Memory and Language*, 57, 163-176.

Hicks, J. A., Cicero, D. C., Trent, J., Burton, C. M., & King, L. A. (2010). Positive affect, intuition, and feelings of meaning. *Journal of Personality and Social Psychology*, 98, 967-979.

Hirsh, J. B., Guindon, A., Morisano, D., & Peterson, J. B. (2010). Positive mood effects on delay discounting. *Emotion*, 10, 717-721.

Hirt, E. R., Devers, E. E., & McCrea, S. M. (2008). I want to be creative: Exploring the role of hedonic contingency theory in the positive mood-cognitive flexibility link. *Journal of Personality and Social Psychology*, 94, 214-230.

Ho, M. Y., Cheung, F. M., & Cheung, S. F. (2010). The role of meaning in life and optimism in promoting well-being. *Personality and Individual Differences*, 48, 658-663.

Holland, R. W., Roeder, U., Van Baaren, R. B., Brandt, A. C., & Hannover, B. (2004). Don't stand so close to me: The effects of self-construal on interpersonal closeness. *Psychological Science*, 15, 237-242.

Hsee, C. K., & Zhang, J. (2004). Distinction bias: Misprediction and mischoice due to joint evaluation. *Journal of Personality and Social Psychology*, 86, 680-695.

Hughes, M., Hughes, P., Mellahi, K., & Guermat, C. (2010). Short-term versus long-term impact of managers: Evidence from the football industry. *British Journal of Management*, 21, 571-589.

James, L. R., McIntyre, M. D., Glisson, C. A., Green, P. D., Patton, T. W., LeBreton, J. M., et al. (2005). Conditional reasoning: An efficient, indirect method for assessing implicit cognitive readiness to aggress. *Organizational Research Methods*, 8, 69-99.

Jordan, A. H., Monin, B., Dweck, C. S., Lovett, B. J., John, O. P., & Gross, J. J. (2011). Misery has more company than people think: underestimating the prevalence of others' negative emotions. *Personality and Social Psychology Bulletin*, 37, 120-135.

Judge, T. A., & Cable, D M. (2011). When it comes to pay, do the thin win? The effect of weight on pay for men and women. *Journal of Applied Psychology*, 96, 95-112.

Karasek, R. (1979). Job demands, job decision latitude, and mental strain. Implications for Job redesign. *Administrative Science Quarterly*, 24, 285-308.

Karremans, J. C., & Aarts, H. (2007). The role of automaticity in determining the inclination to forgive close others. *Journal of Experimental Social Psychology*, 43, 902-917.

Klar, M., & Kasser, T. (2010). Some benefits of being an activist: measuring activism and its role in psychological well-being. *Psychological Science*, 30, 755-777.

Kleisner, K., Kocnar, T., Rubesova, A., & Jaroslav F. (2010). Eye color predicts but does not directly influence perceived dominance in men. *Personality and Individual Differences*, 49, 59-64.

Knight, C., & Haslam, S. A. (2010). Your place or mine? Organizational identification and comfort as mediators of relationships between the managerial control of workspace and employees' satisfaction and well-being. *British Journal of Management*, 21, 717-735.

Kraus, M. W., Huang, C., & Keltner, D. (2010). Tactile communication, cooperation, and performance: An ethological Study of the NBA. *Emotion*, 10, 745-749.

Kross, E., & Ayduk, O. (2008). Facilitating adaptive emotional analysis: Short-term and long-term outcomes distinguishing distanced-analysis of negative emotions from immersed-analysis and distraction. *Personality and Social Psychology Bulletin*, 34, 924-938.

Krumhuber, E., Manstead, S. R., & Kappas, A. (2006). Temporal aspects of facial displays in person and expression perception: the effects of smile dynamics, head-tilt, and gender. *Journal of Nonverbal Behavior*, 31, 39-56.

Kruger, J., Wirtz, D., & Miller, D. T. (2005). Counterfactual thinking and the first instinct fallacy. *Journal of Personality and Social Psychology*, 88, 725-735.

Kuhl, J., & Kazen, M. (2008). Motivation, affect, and hemispheric asymmetry: Power versus affiliation. *Journal of Personality and Social Psychology*, 95, 456-469.

Langens, T. A. (2007). Regulatory focus and illusion of control. *Personality and Social Psychology Bulletin*, 33, 226-237

Leal, S., & Vrij, A. (2008). Blinking during and after lying. *Journal of Nonverbal Behavior*, 32, 187-194.

Lee, L., Amir, O., & Ariely, D. (2009). In search of homo economicus: Cognitive noise and the role of emotion in preference consistency. *Journal of Consumer Research*, 36, 173-187.

Lehmiller, J. L. (2009). Secret romantic relationships: Consequences for personal and relational well-being. *Personality and Social Psychology Bulletin*, 35, 1452-1466.

Levav, J., & Argo, J. J. (2010). Physical contact and financial risk taking. *Psychological Science*, 21, 804-810.

Levav, J., & Zhu, R. (2009). Seeking freedom though variety. *Journal of Consumer Research*, 36, 600-610.

Levine, S. Z., & Jackson, C. J. (2002). Aggregated personality, climate and demographic factors as predictors of departmental shrinkage. *Journal of Business and Psychology*, 17, 287-297.

Li, Y. J., Cohen, A. B., Weeden, J. & Kenrick, D. T. (2010). Mating competitors increase religious beliefs. *Journal of Experimental Social Psychology*, 46, 428-431.

Lichtenfeld, S., Maier, M. A., Elliot, A. J., & Pekrun, R. (2009). The semantic red effect: Processing the word red undermines intellectual performance. *Journal of Experimental Social Psychology*, 45, 1273-1276.

Lilenquist, K., Zhong, C., & Galinsky, A. D. (2010). The smell of virtue: Clean scents promote reciprocity and charity. *Psychological Science*, 21, 381-383.

Maio, G. R., Olson, J. M., Allen, L., & Bernard, M. (2001). Addressing discrepancies between values and behavior: The motivating effect of reasons. *Journal of Experimental Social Psychology*, 37, 104-117.

Markman, K. D., Lindberg, M. J., Kray, L. J., & Galinsky, A. D. (2007). Implications of counterfactual structure for creative generation and analytic problem solving. *Personality and Social Psychology Bulletin*, 33, 312-324.

Mast, M. S., Jonas, K., & Hall, J. A. (2009). Give a person power and he or she will show interpersonal sensitivity: The phenomenon and its why and when. *Journal of Personality and Social Psychology*, 97, 835-850.

Master, S. L., Eisenberger, N. I., Taylor, S. E., Naliboff, B. D., Shirinyan, & Lieberman, M. D. (2009). A picture's worth: Partner photographs reduce experimentally induced pain. *Psychological Science*, 20, 1316-1318.

Masterson, S. S. (2001). A trickle-down model of organizational justice: Relating employees' and customers' perceptions of and reactions to fairness. *Journal of Applied Psychology*, 86, 594-604.

Mayer, N. D., & Tormala, Z. L. (2010). 'Think' versus 'feel' framing effects in persuasion. *Personality and Social Psychology Bulletin*, 36, 443-454.

McKendall, M., DeMarr, B., & Jones-Rikkers, C. (2002). Ethical compliance programs and corporate illegality: Testing the assumptions of the corporate sentencing guidelines. *Journal of Business Ethics*, 37, 367-383.

McNiel, J. M., & Fleeson, W. (2006). The causal effects of extraversion on positive affect and neuroticism on negative affect: Manipulating state extraversion and state neuroticism in an experimental approach. *Journal of Research in Personality*, 40, 529-550.

Meier, B. P., & Robinson, M. D. (2006). Does 'feeling down' mean seeing down? Depressive symptoms and vertical selective attention. *Journal of Research in Personality*, 40, 451-461.

Meier, B. P., Sellbom, M., & Wygant, D. B. (2007). Failing to take the moral high ground: Psychopathy and the vertical representation of morality. *Personality and Individual Differences*, 43, 757-767.

Miller, J. S., & Wiseman, R. M. (2001). Perceptions of executive pay: Does pay enhance a leader's aura. *Journal of Organizational Behavior*, 22, 703-711.

Miller, S. L., Maner, J. K., & Becker, D. V. (2010). Self-protective biases in group categorization: Threat cues shape the psychological boundary between 'us' and 'them'. *Journal of Personality and Social Psychology*, 98, 872-885.

Millward, L. Haslam, S. A., & Postmes, T. (2007). Putting employees in their place: The impact of hot desking on organizational and team identification. *Organization Size*, 18, 547-559.

Minichilli, A., Zattoni, A., & Zona, F. (2009). Making boards effective: an empirical examination of board task performance. *British Journal of Management*, 20, 55-74.

Muris, P., Merckelbach, H., & Horselenberg, R. (1996). Individual differences in thought suppression. The White Bear

Suppression Inventory: Factor structure, reliability, validity and correlates. *Behaviour Research and Therapy*, 34, 501-513.

Nadler, A., Harpaz-Gorodeisky, G., & Ben-David, Y. (2009). Defensive helping: Threat to group identity, ingroup identification, status stability, and common group identity as determinants of intergroup help-giving. *Journal of Personality and Social Psychology*, 97, 823-834.

Nahrgang, J. D., Morgeson, F. P., & Hofmann, D. A. (2011). Safety at work: A meta-analytic investigation of the link between job demands, job resources, burnout, engagement, and safety outcomes. *Journal of Applied Psychology*, 96, 71-94.

Naquin, C. E., Kurtzberg, T. R., & Belkin, L. Y. (2010). The finer points of lying online: e-mail versus pen and paper. *Journal of Applied Psychology*, 95, 387-394.

Neuman, G. A., Wagner, S. H., & Christiansen, N. D. (1999). The relationship between work-team personality composition and the job performance of teams. *Group & Organization Management*, 24, 28-45.

Newcomb, M. D., & Harlow, L. L. (1986). Life events and substance use among adolescents· mediating effects of perceived loss of control and meaningless in life. *Journal of Personality and Social Psychology*, 51, 564-577.

Nicol, A. A. M. (2009). Social Dominance Orientation, Right-Wing Authoritarianism, and their relation with leadership styles. *Personality and Individual Differences*, 47, 657-661.

Nordgren, Banas, K., & MacDonald, G. (2010). Empathy gaps for social pain: Why people underestimate the pain of social suffering, 100, 120-128.

O'Connor Jr., J. P., Priem, R. L., Coombs, J. E., & Gilley, K. M. (2006). Do CEO stock options prevent or promote fraudulent financial reporting? *Academy of Management Journal*, 49, 483-500.

O'Driscol, M. P., Pierce, J. L., & Coghlan, A. (2006). The psychology of ownership: Work environment structure, organizational commitment, and citizenship behaviors. *Group and Organization Management*, 31, 388-416.

Pacini, R., & Epstein, S. (1999). The relation of rational and experiential information processing styles to personality, basic beliefs, and the ratio-bias phenomenon. *Journal of Personality and Social Psychology*, 76, 972-987.

Peetz, J., & Buehler, R. (2009). Is there a budget fallacy? The role of savings goals in the prediction of personal spending. *Personality and Social Psychology Bulletin*, 35, 1579-1591.

Pelham, B. W., Mirrenberg, M. C., & Jones, J. T. (2002). Why Susie sells seashells by the seashore: Implicit egotism and major life decisions. *Journal of Personality and Social Psychology*, 82, 469-487.

Pendry, L., & Carrick, R. (2001). Doing what the mob do: Priming effects on conformity. *European Journal of Social Psychology*, 31, 83-92.

Peterson, R. S., Smith, D. B., Martorana, P. V., & Owens, P. D. (2003). The impact of chief executive officer personality on top management team dynamics: One mechanism by which leadership affects organizational performance. *Journal of Applied Psychology*, 88, 795-808.

Porath, C. L., & Erez, A. (2009). Overlooked but not untouched: How rudeness reduces onlookers' performance on routine and creative tasks. *Organizational Behavior and Human Decision Processes*, 109, 29-44.

Prechel, H., & Morris, T. (2010). The effects of organizational and political embeddedness on financial malfeasance in the largest U. S. corporations: Dependence, incentives, and opportunities. *American Sociological Review*, 75, 331-354.

Pronin, E., Jacobs, E., & Wegner, D. M. (2008). Psychological effects of thought acceleration. Emotion, 8, 597-612.

Pronin, E., Lin, D. Y., & Ross, L. (2002). The bias blind spot: Perceptions of bias in self versus others. *Personality and Social Psychology Bulletin*, 28, 369–381.

Puccinelli, N. M., Tickle-Degnen,L., & Rosenthal, R. (2004). Effect of target position and target task on judge sensitivity to felt rapport. *Journal of Nonverbal Behavior*, 28, 211-220.

Quirin, M., Kazen, M., Rohrman, S., & Kuhl, J. (2009). Implicit but not explicit affectivity predicts circadian and reactive cortisol: Using the implicit positive and negative affect test. *Journal of Personality*, 77, 401-426.

Quoidbach, Dunn, E. W., Petrides, K. V., & Mikolajczak, M. (2010). Money giveth, money taketh away: The dual effect of wealth on happiness. *Psychological Science*, 21, 759-763.

Remus, I., Schind, K. M., Wagner, D. T., Johnson, M. D., DeRue, D. S., & ILgen, D. R. (2007). When can employees have a family life? The effects of daily workload and affect on work-family conflict and social behaviors at home. *Journal of Applied Psychology*, 92, 1368-1379.

Rose, C. L., Murphy, L. B., Byard, L., & Nikzad, K. (2002). The role of the big five personality factors in vigilance performance and workload. *European Journal of Personality*, 16, 185-200.

Rutchick, A. M., Slepian, M. L., & Ferris, B. D. (2010). The pen is mightier than the word: Object priming of evaluative standards. *European Journal of Social Psychology*, 40, 704-708.

Schnall, S., Harber, K. D., Stefanucci, J. K., & Proffitt, D. R. (2008). Social support and the perception of geographical slant. *Journal of Experimental Social Psychology*, 44, 1246-1255.

Schul, Y., Mayo, R., & Burnstein, E. (2004). Encoding under trust and distrust: The spontaneous activation of incongruent cognitions. *Journal of Personality and Social Psychology*, 86, 668-679.

Schwartz, B., Ward, A., Monterosso, J., Lyubomirsky, S., White, K., & Lehman, D. R. (2002). Maximizing versus satisficing: Happiness is a matter of choice. *Journal of Personality and Social Psychology*, 83, 1178-1197.

Scollon, C. N., & Diener, E. (2006). Love, work, and changes in extraversion and neuroticism over time. *Journal of Personality and Social Psychology*, 91, 1152-1165.

Sennett, R. (2006). *The culture of the new capitalism*. New Haven, CT: Yale University Press.

Shantz, A., & Latham, G. P. (2009). An exploratory field experiment on the effect of subconscious and conscious goals on employee performance. *Organizational Behavior and Human Decision Processes*, 109, 9-17.

Sigler, T. H., & Pearson, C. M. (2000). Creating an empowering culture: Examining the relationship between organizational culture and perceptions of empowerment. *Journal of Quality Management*, 5, 27-52.

Simonsohn, U. (2007). Clouds make nerds look good: Field evidence of the impact of incidental factors on decision making. *Journal of Behavioral Decision Making*, 20, 143-152.

Sivanathan, N., Molden, D. C., Galinsky, A. D., & Ku, G. (2008). The promise and peril of self-affirmation in de-escalation of commitment. *Organizational Behavior and Human Decision Processes*, 107, 1-14.

Slepian, M. L., Weisbuch, M., Rutnick, A. M., Newman, L. S., & Ambady, N. (2010). Shedding light on insight: Priming bright ideas. *Journal of Experimental Social Psychology*, 46, 696-700.

Sparrowe, R. T., Soetjipto, B. W., & Kraimer, M. L. (2006). Do leaders' influence tactics relate to members' helping behavior? It depends on the quality of the relationship. *Academy of Management Journal*, 49, 1194-1208.

Sporer, S. L., & Sharman, S. J. (2006). Should I believe this? Reality monitoring of accounts of self-experienced and invented recent and distant autobiographical events. *Applied Cognitive Psychology*, 20, 837-854.

Stillman, T. F., Baumeister, R. F., Lambert, N. M., Crescioni, A. W., DeWall, C. D., & Fincham, F. D. (2009). Alone and without purpose: Life loses meaning following social exclusion. *Journal of Experimental Social Psychology*, 45, 686-694.

Thompson, C. A. Beauvais, L. L., & Lyness, K. S. (1999). When work-family benefits are not enough: The influence of work-family culture on benefit utilization, organizational attachment, and work-family conflict. *Journal of Vocational Behavior*, 54, 392-415.

Uziel, L. (2007). Individual differences in the social facilitation effect: A review and meta-analysis. *Journal of Research in Personality*, 41, 579-601.

Van Dillen, L. & Koole, S. L. (2007). Clearing the mind: A working memory model of distraction from negative mood. *Emotion*, 7, 715-723.

Van Tongreen, D., & Green, J. D. (2010). Combating meaninglessness: On the automatic defense of meaning. *Personality and Social Psychology Bulletin*, 36, 1372-1384.

Vrij, A., Akehurst, L., & Morris, P. (1997). Individual differences in hand movements during deception. *Journal of Nonverbal Behavior*, 21, 87-102.

Vrij, A., Edward, K., & Bull, R. (2001). Stereotypical verbal and nonverbal responses while deceiving others. *Personality & Social Psychology Bulletin*, 27, 899-909.

Vrij, A., Pannell, H., & Ost, J. (2005). The influence of social pressure and black clothing on crime judgements. *Psychology, Crime, & Law*, 11, 3, 265-274.

Wan, E. W., & Sternthal, B. (2008). Regulating the effects of depletion through monitoring. *Personality and Social Psychology Bulletin*, 34, 32-46.

Wang, P., & Walumbwa, F. O. (2007). Family-friendly programs, organizational commitment, and work withdrawal: The moderating role of transformational leadership. *Personnel Psychology*, 60, 397-427.

Warneken, F., & Tomasello, M. (2008). Extrinsic rewards undermine altruistic tendencies in 20-month-olds. *Developmental Psychology*, 44, 1785-1788.

Warren, G., Schertler, E., & Bull, P. (2010). Detecting deception from emotional and unemotional cues. *Journal of Nonverbal Behavior*, 33, 59-69.

Wichman, A. L., Brinol, P., Petty, R. E., Rucker, D. D., & Tormala, Z. L. (2010). Doubting one's doubt: A formula for confidence? *Journal of Experimental Social Psychology*, 46, 350-355.

Wilson, T. D., Centerbar, D. B., Kermer, D. A., & Gilbert, D. T. (2005). The pleasures of uncertainty: Prolonging positive moods in ways people do not anticipate. *Journal of Personality and Social Psychology*, 88, 5-21.

Wilson, T., & Gilbert, D. T. (2003). Affective forecasting. *Advances in Experimental Social Psychology*, 35, 345-411.

Wilson, T. D., & Gilbert, D. T. (2005). Affective forecasting: Knowing what to want. *Current Directions in Psychological Science*, 14, 131-134.

Wood, S. (2010). The comfort food fallacy: Avoiding old favorites in times of change. *Journal of Consumer Research*, 36, 950-963.

Zhang, Y., Feick, L., & Price, L. J. (2006). The impact of self construal on aesthetic preference for angular versus rounded shapes. *Personality and Social Psychology Bulletin*, 32, 794-805.

Zhong, C., & DeVoe, S. E. (2010). You are how you eat: Fast food and impatience. *Psychological Science*, 21, 619-622.

Zhou, J., & George, J. M. (2001). When job dissatisfaction leads to creativity: Encouraging the expression of voice. *Academy of Management Journal*, 44, 682-696.

Zyglidopoulos, S. C. (2005). The impact of downsizing on corporate reputation. *British Journal of Management*, 16, 253-259.

Index

Where Should I Work?